THE ASSAULT

ALLEN R. MATTHEWS wrote this grim but truthful story of a foot soldier's existence shortly after being evacuated from the island of Iwo Jima. Recovering from extreme exhaustion in a U.S. medical facility on Guam, recalling how chance had spared his life while taking the lives of so many of his comrades, he found war far from the glamorous Hollywood film. War, he said, was "a foul business full of fear and loneliness and misery."

Matthews was born in Macon, Georgia. After graduating from Mercer University in 1935, he began a career as journalist, joining the Richmond *Times-Dispatch* in 1940. He entered the Marine Corps in 1944 and was assigned to the Fourth Marine Division. After the war he returned briefly to journalism before becoming Executive Vice President of the Jamestown Corporation in Virginia. The father of three sons, Matthews died in 1957. His widow is now a librarian at Mercer University.

THE ASSAULT

Allen R. Matthews

DODD, MEAD & COMPANY
NEW YORK

Printed in the United States of America

1 2 3 4 5 6 7 8 9 10

Library of Congress Cataloging in Publication Data

Matthews, Allen R
  The assault.

  Originally published in 1947 by Simon and Schuster, New York.
  1. Iwo Jima, Battle of, 1945—Personal narratives,
American. 2. Matthews, Allen R. 3. United States.
Army—Biography. 4. Soldiers—United States—Biography.
I. Title.
D767.99.I9M3   1980   940.54'26   80-14926
ISBN 0-396-07874-5
ISBN 0-396-07875-3 (pbk.)

THE
ASSAULT

1

I was tired. My muscles ached and my joints hurt and I could not co-ordinate my mind and my actions. As I walked, being half-led and half-carried into the reception ward, my knees snapped back and then buckled forward uncontrollably.

My mind and my body seemed disconnected, as if they were standing apart one from the other, each glaring at the other in impotent confusion. *And the sand and the cold and the hunger and the lazy gluttonous huge blue and green flies on their throats and mouths and the odor of alcohol and the hardness of the steel deck under my feet and the bright glare of the lights over the man's head and my foot my foot why didn't it stop hurting and the grace-noted* sing-whack-whop *of a bullet close overhead and the sand, the everlasting sand in your mouth and teeth and ears and eyes and worse still in your rifle and the ants and the food where was the food and where were the Japs and . . .*

"I'm going to try as much as possible to keep this from hurting you," but he did not succeed.

The sight of the scalpel in the man's hands was as

remote as if I were viewing it through the wrong end of a telescope; and so was my thumb, into which the scalpel cut, until the hurt began and then it viciously rejoined my body and my mind. Strange, no blood; everything was blood and sand. And hurt. The hurt made it authentic.

In the distance through the crazy telescope which wasn't there, a medical corpsman cut off my leggings but thoughtfully untied my shoes. He removed my socks, and the doctor, all in that moment a matter of wispy red hair, a comforting paunch, and cool, gentle hands, looked at the aching foot. No medication was applied and his only comment was a grunt. He turned to a boy across the way, from the side of whose head blood still flowed beneath a loosely applied unbleached battle dressing.

"Would you like to leave your valuables with us?" It was the corpsman again.

He helped me fumble through the pockets of my uniform. I left my valuables: my pen knife with the fingernail file on it and my other pen knife with the trick sliding blade, my billfold which was empty, and eleven cents in change, the brush with which I had tried vainly to keep my rifle free of sand, the tiny leather folder containing pictures of my wife and son and my waggish neighbor who had insisted on posing in full-length profile when she was pregnant. And I left my fountain pen which had lost its ink from concussion during the first five days, and a package of rifle cleaning patches, four of which remained. And I left my piece of shrapnel. The piece of shrapnel which struck me in the center of the back on the fifth day with force enough to throw me to my knees but without the power (it was broad and long and had hit me flat) to do

2

more than scratch the surface of the skin. Of these was my world of property built.

With the corpsman's arm encircling my body I shuffled to the passageway leading to the ship's hospital quarters, teetered back precariously to allow the entrance of four men bearing a stretcher case and then went forward again.

So the first squad of the second platoon was gone. It was gone, by ones and twos, but irrevocably, and in leaving, each member had removed not only himself but a piece of those who remained behind him. It was a truth never more apparent than in battle. The last of the other twelve had been exhausted two days ago and some were dead and some were wounded and some sick and some injured. But they were gone and now I was gone also.

I came down off the ridge in midafternoon of the twelfth day. I ran and walked until, completely exhausted, I fell and crawled across the calf-deep ash-sand of the open terrain to the precarious safety of a razorbacked hillock where only two days earlier a sniper's bullet had felled the big, red-faced, drawling L——.

My chest was so constricted that I breathed shallowly and rapidly. My heart pounded so fiercely from the exertion that my face felt hot and puffy and the skin on either side of my nose seemed to be stretched until it had pulled from its foundation.

The group of men leaning heavily on their weapons or merely lying behind the hillock stared at me sullenly and thought—because they always thought it when they saw you were unhurt—*what are you doing here you're not hit God damn it move on this is our shelter*

3

and one more is too many and you'll draw fire. They didn't say it, but they thought it.

I fought for my breath and said: "Where is the First Battalion c.p.?"

The men looked at me uncomprehendingly. No one attempted to answer. I turned to a jeep driver who, goggled against the blinding dust, strained at unloading his ammunition-filled trailer.

"Do *you* know where the c.p. is?"

"You bet. Hell, I'm going by it in just a few minutes; it's our c.p., too. Just hop in the seat there and I'll be ready to go down in a few minutes."

I couldn't hop. I crawled into the seat and braced my right foot against the fender.

"Do you have a cigarette? . . . I haven't had a whole cigarette in hours."

"Yeh. Here, help yourself. No, go on and take the pack. I can get all I want and you may be a long time in finding any more."

I remonstrated feebly, but I took the almost full package, because I wanted cigarettes. I could, I had thought a hundred times during the last five days, get along without food and I could do without a great deal of water but God! not the cigarettes.

The jeep driver and his helper worked busily unloading cans of 60-millimeter mortar ammunition. Their chore completed, they climbed into the jeep, backed around so that the trailer protruded from behind the hillock into the flat open space facing the Japanese lines, and shot forward into the ruts which constituted the road leading down to the beach.

I moved my foot from the fender to the floorboard and clutched tightly to the back of the seat with my left

4

hand. We rushed around a sharp curve, bounding crazily, and came to a sliding halt.

Ahead was a small group of men plodding toward the rear.

"Would you look at this?" the driver demanded. "They let their f——g casualties walk all the way back to the aid station because they're too gutless to send a jeep up on the ridge."

He clashed his gears angrily and drove forward slowly, drawing alongside the men who were walking in three pairs, each pair consisting of a wounded man supported by a comrade.

"Here, put those people in the back there. That one can get in the trailer. . . . Why don't you give your jeep drivers the word? They can do this as well as I can. They want this outfit's jeeps to do all their work for them. I'm going to knock it off."

He spat into the dust alongside the trail, ground his gears again as the silent men boarded the vehicle, and we bounced forward once more, the driver still muttering his disdain for his fellow drivers.

We halted a few minutes later in front of what evidently was a command and aid post and the driver cut his motor so that the sounds which were the past became again the present. The anger of the battlefield now to our left was a snarl and a rumble, a din which we heard only when it was gone or when it was punctuated violently. The noise was a part of our existence as much as were the foul air and the dirty water and the obscene words and the no-food. These were everything and nothing; they were a part of time, but that meant nothing also. For time was now two-dimensional. It had its *past* which somehow trespassed

5

into the *now* to become the present but there was nothing of the *future* in our existence. We had our length and breadth which were instincts and sensation, but we lacked entirely the depth which was understanding. Time, the basis of understanding, was a lifetime wrapped in a few days. The years which had gone before were meaningless except for their contribution to sensation: the sudden sharp memory of hot food or the exquisite realization of the meaning of warm water. The future simply was not there, either in our living or our planning. When we managed to get an extra pack of cigarettes, we did so not for the future but because we needed them yesterday. We threw away our gas masks not because we would not need them tomorrow; we merely didn't need them yesterday.

The driver looked over his shoulder. "Okay, you fellows, here's your c.p. . . .

"Not yours," he added to me as I put a foot outside the jeep. I drew it in again. "We'll be there in just a few minutes.

"Hey, you people," he shouted in the direction of the aid station, "got any cases going to the beach? I'm going down there right now. . . . For Christ's sake, look at that."

A few men, obviously recently wounded, were staggering into the post from another direction.

"Don't they bring any of 'em down?"

Obviously they did, for two ambulance jeeps were drawn up near a huge shell crater and corpsmen were lifting stretchers from them as we watched. But out driver chose to ignore that, even though he drove his jeep ahead to make way for the other two vehicles to leave. He turned back to me.

6

"It's been hell up there, hasn't it?" His voice was now amiably conversational.

I said hell was an understatement.

"You should've seen the men that've been coming down the last five days. It's a wonder there's anybody left."

A boy, obviously still in his teens, was hoisted up from the shell crater and dragged, then carried, to our jeep. Tears streamed down his face leaving clean tracks through the dust and grime which had gathered there for days.

"I won't! I won't!" his voice rose to a wail. "God *damn* it, I won't." His wails suddenly broke and he began a hiccoughing sob, "I won't—won't—won't. . . ."

His comrades lifted him by the arms and legs and dropped him over the side of the jeep trailer into its bottom.

"One of you people climb in there with him. I can't take him down there like that without somebody to watch him," the driver said. One of the two comrades climbed over the edge and sat beside the casualty.

"I won't! I won't!" the boy suddenly screamed again. His companion clutched him by the upper arm.

"Now, Jerry, you'll be all right. That's a good boy, Jerry, you'll be all right." He spoke soothingly, almost in a crooning voice and the boy's screams again subsided into sobs. Two other patients walked over unassisted and climbed into the trailer. We started forward again.

That's a good boy, Jerry, you'll be all right and you'll be off here in five days and the cooks are landing too and in a day or so you'll have hot food brought to you just like on maneuvers and you can have anything in the way of new equipment you want just so long as it ain't more than one pair of cotton socks and my feet are like a coupla fish been dead five days and if you could only see the Japs that'd be something. . . .

The driver's voice came through again:

"There's the c.p. over there. Do you see it?" he pointed to a group of men and vehicles drawn close under the protecting side of a cliff. I nodded. He slowed and began to turn in the direction of the command post.

"For God's sake, don't turn in there," his helper said. "It's too damned hard to get out once you're in. I think this man's strong enough to walk up there— aren't you? It's just a short way."

I nodded again, the driver halted the vehicle and I stepped out, thanked him for the ride and the cigarettes. He waved his hand, said, "Take it easy," and drove off. I waited until the jeep had gotten under way again, then shuffled up the dusty trail, unable to lift my feet completely off the ground. I was, I felt, going to fall to pieces. *If I could just sit down.*

Again I was a jeep passenger, but this time I sat in the trailer; I had been tagged, unexpectedly, for evacuation to the beach. Occupying the trailer with me was a red-haired, white-faced boy, his cheeks so smooth that it was evident he shaved seldom, if ever. He was unwounded, but the tag hanging from his jacket read in boldly scrawled lettering, "Dysentery."

"Where've you been?" he asked.

"Ridge."

"Lose many?"

"Everybody. Almost. I was the last man in my squad. When I left there were only four men in my

8

platoon and only two of those hit the beach with us.''

''God.''

We sat silent for a few moments.

''We were shot to hell, too. We didn't have anybody left.''

He subsided again. Then his face contorted. He began to weep.

''This God damn dysentery!''

He was being irrelevant and I knew it. Then he abandoned all pretense.

''They send you up to a place like that and you get shot to hell and maybe they pull you back. But they send you right up again and then you get murdered. God, you stay there until you get killed or until you can't stand it any more.''

He was on the verge of a crack-up. I patted his knee ineffectually once or twice, then stopped. I, too, had an almost overwhelming desire to cry.

We were helped out of the jeep at the beach evacuation station. A corpsman led each of us into a long, low tent where a few men sat drinking coffee out of ration cans. We lay in the dust—the tent was floorless—and the men put aside their coffee and filed by, stooping to read and copy the information on our evacuation tags. Their work completed, they offered us cigarettes, gave us two sedative tablets each, and offered us individual bars of tropical chocolate (chocolate unaffected by the normal heat of the tropics) which were approximately the size of those sold in the States in prewar days for a cent each.

My head swam drunkenly when I stood up to climb into the wheeled, amphibious ''Duck'' which stopped in front of the evacuation tent to remove the casualties to the ship. The corpsman who had given me the candy helped me up a ladder and over the side of the vehicle, climbing laboriously after me and supporting me with his hands on my hips. My dizziness passed as we headed into the water, the first wave picking us up and setting us down hard on the sandy floor of the ocean. The second crest lifted us high again and this time we roared free.

Eight casualties occupied the craft. Five of us were ambulatory, the other three, stretcher cases. My red-haired companion was not among us.

Several hundred yards offshore the "Duck" was lashed to a Higgins boat and we were transferred. The Higgins boat then drew alongside the mother ship, cables were passed down, and the craft was jerked out of the water by derricks. We rose to a level with the deck of the larger ship and again we were transferred.

This was haven and sanctuary. This was good food and sleep. (How long had it been since I had had a night's uninterrupted sleep?) This was cleanliness. Here was neither shell fire nor mortar bursts nor thirst nor loneliness by day nor the terror of night. Here was the comfort of solicitous friends—friends you didn't know, and those you did.

For here were some I had known, and they grinned and spoke to me out of the dead where they must have been but were not now. Here were three who had been marked missing after the rocket bomb had struck.

There was Merrill, who had been standing with M—— when M—— had been struck so grievously by the bomb that he had died shortly afterward. And there, grinning from his bunk was the giant Savage, the new corporal who had joined our platoon only three days before he was hit by fragments from the same missile. After the explosion he could not be found, but then neither could Doc Scala, the Navy medical corpsman who had been with the Fourth Division so long he considered himself more a marine than a sailor. There, too, was Scala. He limped over and put his arm about me as I came into the compartment.

The corpsman led me to a berth and there, in another above it, lay Boudrie the platoon guide; also in the compartment was the corporal, Kennedy, who came and gripped my hand. The corpsman waved my friends away, telling them to return in the morning. He poured me a cup of coffee, refilled it three times. He helped me out of my dungarees and led me into the adjoining head where I propped myself in a shower stall and let the wonderful warm water stream over me.

I don't recall crumpling onto the berth.

2

A long time ago I could remember when we gathered in the early evenings on the fantail of our LST (landing ship, tanks). Then, comfortably filled with night chow, we listened to four crewmen get in what they called, too ambitiously, the groove. There was the tall, rugged machinist with his xylophone, the guitar player, the clarinetist, and the saxophonist. We understood that they weren't competent musicians—we should have been outraged had we heard the same group on a stage—but in the informality of the immediate present they were good. Everything was good. And we laughed and applauded after each of their numbers; shouting suggestions for encores.

Even when the public address system sounded: "Now hear this: the smoking lamp is out; all hands darken ship," we clung to those last few seconds of the fading light for more music. For the music was fellowship and laughter and we had much of both to give and to receive. We stayed on deck, that is, until the appetite for another smoke drove us into the deckhouse or below to our compartments, for when does anyone crave a cigarette more than at the time when he knows he cannot have another?

I remember, too, when the crewman called Frankie (that wasn't his name, but because he sang he had it painted, along with a bar of treble-clef music, across the back of his blue denim work shirts) sang that parody on the popular song, Argentina.

> "You know your life will begin
> The very moment you're in
> Iwo Jima. . . ."

How we laughed when he sang it, for life was good and we—the new ones, at least—felt tough and invincible and somehow indestructible.

We talked about the song again on D-day, I remember.

M—— said: "That song should have gone:

> 'You know your life will just end
> The very moment you're in
> Iwo Jima. . . .' "

We laughed again then, but our laughter had scant humor in it.

I remember, too, the night when big Steve Turlo, the sergeant and squad leader, lay on his sack in the troop compartment and asked:

"How do you guys feel about this operation; I mean, do you think it's gonna be tough or easy?" And then he directed his question to me personally, "How about you, Matchu?" Turlo was a Polack (his name was shortened from Stefanetti Turlovowski) but he had

14

been reared in a northern part of Maine which had caught an overflow of French Canadians, so that he spoke with something of a French accent and he had trouble with his th's; they became d's or t's or, in the case of my name, ch's.

I looked at him for a moment without replying. It was a question I had asked myself for days without getting a satisfactory answer.

"I think it's going to be tough," I finally answered. He looked at me closely for a few seconds.

"How about you, Middleditch?"

"I think it's going to be a snap," said Middleditch. "Nothing to it."

"You do?" Turlo grinned widely. He liked Middleditch and so did the rest of the squad, for Middleditch, Bronx-born and reared (I remember how he sidled around a herd of harmless milk cows on a practice march out of camp one day), had no inhibitions and no regard for rank or prestige. Furthermore, he sang abominable songs in a screeching falsetto which set your hair on end. He also sang at the drop of a hat.

"Sure I do. We've been knocking hell out of them with our air force for more than a month now. And our fleet is going to keep reinforcements out. They give us five days to secure the island; I think it'll be over in three."

"How about you, Miley; what do you think?"

Miley grinned that beaming, eye-closing grin of his and said:

"I don't know, Turlo; I'll be damned if I know."

"Well, Matchu," he looked at me again, "how do you *feel* about this? I mean, do you feel nervous, scared, or cool, or what?"

"No, Turlo," I replied. "I'm not scared, or nervous. I haven't even seen anyone on board who appears to be that way. Nervousness and fear are contagious, don't you think?" He agreed by nodding. "And when it sets in with a man among a group of men like this you can feel it; it gets so thick you can almost cut it with a knife. I've seen it and I've felt it grow in a crowd.

"When you asked a few minutes ago how I felt about the campaign, I said it was going to be tough, but I don't know. I'm too ignorant about the whole business, to tell you the truth. I suppose that everybody going into action tries to tell himself how he'll react; I suspect few succeed. They tried to train us for this sort of thing by firing artillery and machine guns over us, but that didn't mean anything. Everybody knew then that they were *trying* to miss us. There must be a hell of a big difference in being shot *at* when you know the shooter means business.

"I've thought about it a lot in the last few days and I can tell you what I *think:* I think that on D-day I'll be scared—scared as hell. I'll probably go into the beach shaking like a dog shittin' peach seeds. But I think—I hope—that the longer I stay on the island the less scared I'll be. I may just play a shaky follow-the-leader the first day or so, but I believe I'll be all right after that.

"I said it was going to be tough for another reason, too." I was getting loquacious and afterward I wondered if that might not have been a sign of nervousness which I didn't recognize. "I've found out that if I paint things in my mind just as black as possible, they don't ever turn out to be quite so bad as I had imagined them. So I'm telling myself that the operation is going to be almost unbearably tough."

16

I was a fool, you see. My mind could not conceive the horrors of such a campaign and the passage of the first day of fighting did little good, for it continued to get worse.

And I recall the church service atop the deckhouse on D-day-minus-one. Nervousness *was* in the air then so that you almost had to fight through it as you walked along the deck. You thought then, certainly, that almost all the company would attend, but it was a surprisingly small congregation, perhaps 100 men, perhaps less.

It was a simple service, led by the ship's executive officer who stood with his back to the stern, his feet braced wide against the rolling of the flat-bottomed craft. The ship and sea noises forced him to speak into a small hand microphone and his words came almost diffidently, lending a kind of dignity to the service.

This time, the first since we had left our base, he omitted the sermon which heretofore he had read from a small religious pamphlet.

Instead he, together with the congregation, intoned in singsong fashion the Twenty-third Psalm:

"The Lord . . . is my shepherd . . . I shall . . . not want. . . ."

And to the magnificent words of faith:

"Yea, though I walk . . . through the valley . . . of the shadow of death . . . I shall fear . . . no evil . . . for Thou art with me . . . Thy rod . . . and Thy staff . . . they comfort me. . . . "

That was the essence of the service, which lasted barely fifteen minutes. The executive officer read a prayer which asked for the strength of faith, but conspicuously made no plea for a saving hand in the coming struggle, and the service ended with the singing, much off-key—for the officer forgot to use his microphone with the result that those in the rear plunged in independently—of "What a Friend We Have in Jesus."

And a friend and I wondered aloud to each other about the service and about the few persons attending. On that day, of all days, I had thought the deckhouse would be overflowing.

It was rather strange in view of the troops' avid turning, only a day or two previously, to the Ouija board. I remember that, and how many of them were shamefacedly insistent about how much the board could tell them:

"Why, it went straight to the number of this ship when we asked it."

Or, from one who had manipulated it:

"And it knew my middle name."

"And it said I would be a casualty but not killed."

"It told me that the campaign would last four days."

Hadn't Vic Heyden the Coast Guard correspondent been wrong the night he sat in his tiny office and interviewed four of the men who had what they thought were good results from the Ouija board? He said then:

"I guess a lot of guys will be getting religion all of a sudden. All this stress and strain. But I'll be damned if I believe in that old crap about there being no atheists in foxholes. As an atheist," and he grinned up at the uncomfortable Marines in front of him, "I think I'll form a Foxhole Atheists Society, to protest the statement of that chaplain.

"Of course, I don't really know. You put me in a tough spot like some of you fellows have been in and I might pray too. Something like, 'Oh God, I really don't believe You're there but if You *are* there, it'd be mighty

18

white of You to help me out right now . . . '

"Of course, that's just a sort of insurance—death insurance, let's say."

The Marines looked bemused. Bob Warren, the Coast Guard combat photographer, glared at him, exasperated.

"I don't think he's an atheist at all. He just likes to hear himself talk."

Eight days later my friend and foxhole companion said:

"Boy, I never thought we'd come out of that one. I prayed the whole time."

So did I. . . .

And the skies swayed beyond the masts of the ship and the weather stayed mild and we exercised every day and ate enormously and we read and shot the shit and cleaned our rifles and pitied the first platoon which had inspections in addition to its exercises and we played rummy and pinochle and poker and read mostly lewd books and the days ran one into the other until time became meaningless and the sun stood still and space became everything.

But once in awhile someone would get serious and portentously dramatic and say it's hard to realize (this coming when several were gathered in a bull session) that some of us probably aren't coming back, and some wit would retort almost inevitably *well I'll be around to piss on your grave.*

We became strategic and military once in awhile, too, and they dragged out the maps and the timetables and they said the island will be secured in five days and there'll be five more days of mopping up and *this is the OA line where you'll go when you hit the beach after*

19

you hit the beach here at Blue Beach One and A and B companies will be in front of you and the Third Battalion on their right and the Twenty-third on your left and the O-1 and the ships will stop 4,000 yards from the beach and the LD will be 1,500 yards from the shore and 25 bombers and 25 fighters will hit the ridge at H-minus-10 and the ships will begin an intense bombardment on D-minus-three and continue through D-day and on D-day they'll put down a rolling barrage hitting the beach until H-hour and then shift their targets inland 100 yards every five minutes until they knock out all the Jap fire in front of you and pin down the rest and we're going to give you an exam on all this (you'd better study hard, we told each other; if you flunk they may not let you go in with the assault).

Except they forgot to tell the Japs about being pinned down. And they forgot to tell us when to duck.

3

But, after all, you've got to learn something for your-self, and ducking is an easy lesson if you are fortunate enough to be an apt pupil.

And maybe they did forget to tell you how to avoid the ants and the flies and what to do when the foxhole persisted in caving in on top of you and how to eat beef and vegetable stew out of a can with a combat knife—when you could get the stew to eat.

Not all of it was bum scoop, however.

On D-minus-two night we found out why they had insisted that we bring our flannel shirts and our combat jackets. They had told us—to our considerable disbe-lief, for on the map Iwo still looked pretty far south—that the average temperature was around 40 degrees. But they didn't say what the 40 degrees was the aver-age for: the month, the year, the season, day and night, or just night.

I, being cautious, also brought a sleeveless khaki wool sweater and a sweat shirt.

Not until D-minus-two night did we have any

foretaste of cool weather. But that night, without warning and as soon as the sun had sunk out of sight off to the port, it turned achingly cool and the men who had been sleeping topside scurried below to the warmth of the troop compartments.

On Sunday when I filled my pack, therefore, I withheld my flannel shirt and my combat jacket—more clothing, I felt, might only make me awkward—to be worn with my dungarees.

By midafternoon of Sunday I was ready to go. My pack had been stowed with the others which later were to be deposited on the beach and I had only what were considered the bare necessities: my clean dungarees dipped two days before in an insect repellent and soap mixture, my best shoes, two pairs of woolen socks, a handkerchief, skivvy shirt and drawers, my helmet, a dangerously sharpened bayonet, my combat knife, my cartridge belt loaded with ten clips of armor-piercing ammunition, four fragmentation hand grenades which I carried in an assistant BAR-men's belt, two canteens of water, my first aid pouch, my leggings, and my gas mask.

It was, we all supposed, the time for writing, and most of us scribbled short notes to those at home but I never mailed mine, for even the ordinary things which I would have said in any other letter seemed inappropriate in this one. And I thought: my wife will get this letter probably while the operation still is underway and before she has heard whether I am safe. Will even a simple message of love seem over-written—or under-written—and will she think I am excited?

I saw that I had lost all power to see myself through my letters as I should have liked to have others see me; I merely folded the two sheets of paper and put them away. It was, I thought, perhaps the time to write what might be a last letter, but I could not bring myself to do so. That kind of letter, in which I could point out all the dire possibilities, would be much more aptly timed if it were not written when the possibilities were so mathematically exacting.

Instead, I lay on my sack and, as did so many others that afternoon, looked at the bottom of the sack above me and at the people passing and at my hands and at the rifle in its weather cover at the head of my sack and I thought thoughts; what they were I may have known at the time, but I do not now, nor would I have then had anyone asked me within seconds of their contemplation. Doubtless they should have been of eternity or infinity or my place in things, but they were no more important than: will I be able to eat my next meal with an appearance of gusto so that nobody will see I'm as nervous as I feel.

I strolled the deck and lay in the sun and the members of the crew passed by and spoke in a new subdued sort of way and I wasn't comfortable there and returned to the troop compartment and tried again to rest. But rest is sleep and sleep could not be induced then.

At night they turned on the fresh water in the showers so that we could go ashore clean and germ-resistant. Since fresh water was as a priceless jewel to us they had to assign showers and times by platoons and we all washed and felt better for it.

Supper that night was the usual Sunday night chow: horse-cock (cold cuts, that is), beans, and potato salad with olives as a fillip and I surprised myself by eating with pleasure. But not everyone had my appetite and the GI cans at the door to the mess hall were filled with unconsumed food. It was simply a repetition of the scene which occurred after the noon chow of smothered chicken and dressing and candied sweet potatoes and salad and peas and pie. They fed us well on D-minus-one and it was a standing joke, which suddenly had turned macabre, that they liked to fatten us up for the slaughter.

After supper it was Smokey Morrison, the corporal, and Jimmie Matchunis, the private, both of Richmond, who suggested that we meet again in the mess hall afterward. When it was cleared the mess hall also served as game and reading room. Smokey and I were there, but Matchunis failed to arrive—the next day he explained that he had fallen asleep. We were there not to play games or to read. We merely talked for a few minutes and then we exchanged addresses of our respective wives in case, we said, one of us returns to the States before the other. But we were evading the issue and we both knew it, for we were exchanging the addresses not only of our wives but of our next-of-kin who could be notified by something more personal than a government telegram should anything happen to either of us.

Together with Ray Marine, who had been with me since boot camp, Morrison and I strolled on the chilly weather deck, for it was now late, and we tried to see something of Iwo Jima but we still were too far away.

We separated and I stopped for a chat with Vic Heyden, the correspondent, and Bob Warren, the photographer, but they were no help. Their minds were full of tomorrow also and they were so polite to me that I felt they already were committing the corpse, so I fled and returned to my compartment. I hit the sack fully clothed and must have fallen asleep quickly for I awoke only with the sound of reveille which in our case was no bugle call but the turning on of lights and the cry "Hit the deck! Hit the deck!" Most of us ignored the call and stayed in our sacks until others in nearby compartments began to go through to morning chow nearly an hour later.

Not until then did we arise, splash our faces and hands in cold water, brush our teeth, and join the chow line which formed below deck. The food, like that of yesterday, was good: grapefruit, two eggs fried sunnyside, and thick ham steaks. I ate all my chow, but my appetite was not as good as it had been and I knew that I was forcing myself to eat.

And the realization, which had only pricked my consciousness from the outside, intruded boldly now: this is D-day; "this," in the words of that dramatic officer back in the States "is *it!*"

I went topside after chow. It was dark yet, but in the distance could be seen an occasional flash of an exploding shell and the long graceful red arc of missiles fired from the big guns of warships.

It was too early, however, for anything definite to be seen and I returned to the compartment. I was shivering from the piercing cold of the weather deck, and the warmth of the compartment was good. But it was not enough to hold me below deck, and when the word came down that "that volcano" was visible, our compartment emptied topside with a rush.

Suribachi, "that volcano," was visible and so was most of the remainder of the island. Iwo is, as one member of the platoon described it, shaped like a pork chop. Suribachi stood out, magnificent and menacing, at the extreme tip of the small end. Stretching northeast to where the meaty portion of the chop would be, was the beach on which we were to land. The meaty portion itself stood in crags and cliffs rising abruptly off the right flank of the beach. From the beach, the land lifted itself in a series of rapid terraces to the point where the bone of the chop should be. At this point on the lower half of the island lay Motoyama airport number one, first and greatest immediate objective of the attacking force, and to the attackers' right when facing the airport was the taxiway connecting this, the largest airfield on the island, with Motoyama airport number two.

Tom Kennedy, the corporal and assistant squad leader, stood with me near the bow of our ship, both of us straining our eyes at this area, for somewhere along this runway was a revetment—*"Now from where we land on this beach it will be easy to line up this cross road here with the first revetment on the right of the taxiway there and it will be easy to make your way there, where we will turn right and start our push up the island."*

In the morning's slight haze and the heavy pall of smoke which hung over the island it was *not* easy to line up the two points; they could not even be seen with the naked eye from the ship. The pounding which the island took at the hands of our bombers and naval craft was such, in fact, that I not only never saw the revetment and the cross road in relation to each other; I never saw either point to recognize it as such.

We looked in vain, too, to determine the extent of our first immediate natural hazard: a terrace of boggy ash sand which wound, at varying heights and angles of acclivity, along the beach only a few yards from the water's edge. We had been told that if the terrace were low enough, and its slope gentle, we should be trans-

26

ported inland as far as possible in our amphibious tractors; otherwise, we should be forced out by the ocean and made to run for it.

The air was full of the short flat cracks of the ship gunfire and the island looked almost like an exhausted quarry at bay in the midst of a ring of yapping, snarling dogs. The warships encircled the small bit of land and they roared their anger in the varying pitches of their guns.

"Do you see any battlewagons?" I asked and Kennedy pointed southwest of Suribachi where a huge ship thrust out a long tongue of flame at the island and three shells carved a graceful red arc through the sky and seconds later the sound of the discharge reached our ears almost as one loud crash.

Then I saw the shape of other battleships and of cruisers and the low sleek lines of destroyers and the air was filled with the strange thumping whacking whistling cacophony of the barrage and the coldness was forgotten in the excitement of the attack. Goose flesh persisted, but not from the chill air.

And the troops packed tight along the rails exchanged what they hoped were carefree smiles with one another and they said *they're really pouring it in, ain't they* and *I'd rather be out here going in than in there having to go through what they're going through* and someone said *I wonder if we're still drawing fire from shore batteries* and the grins disappeared with the thought and we all turned more anxious eyes toward the island.

Midway up the island from the beach something flickered twice like the signal lights from a warship and I pointed out the spot to Kennedy.

"What are those? Are they explosions of our shells

or the muzzle blasts from Jap guns?"

"I don't know, but I believe they must be the explosions of our shells. You can bet though that they haven't knocked out all the Jap guns. I just hope that they don't say anything about not having any targets. If they don't I'll feel better. I remember on Saipan that they said the 16-inch guns didn't have any more targets and then they said there weren't any for the eight-inch guns, and then for the five-inchers. But when we went into the beach—wham! all hell broke loose."

I went below to the head and I took my place in the line which stretched into the adjoining compartment and the line was as long as a beer line back in camp and we joked about it although we were a little embarrassed secretly by this show of the frailty of our nerves and someone said that Scott Paper Company ought to be able to declare a big dividend if we have many more operations. But others were less considerate of themselves and their acquaintances and passed along the line saying "What! are you back again? You must have gotten rid of your teeth by now." And it was true; many *had* returned again and again.

I returned to the weather deck and found Kennedy still there, but the crowd about the bow rails had begun to thin away and Turlo passed by, shouting;

"Kennedy! Matchu! Be in the tank deck by seven-fifteen. You better get your gear on. You don't have long. Seen Seiden?" And without waiting for a reply he hurried off.

Kennedy and I turned back and clattered down the ladder to our compartment and again I had a strong recurrence of the this-is-it feeling and the tenseness in the compartment was something almost tangible. The men, silent, shrugged their way into their gear, buck-

28

led their cartridge belts, and picked up their rifles and BARs and walked, bulky and awkward looking, toward the hatch leading onto the tank decks and then returned to make certain they had forgotten nothing.

I slipped my hands through the belt suspenders which helped distribute the weight of my loaded cartridge belt to my shoulders as well as on my hips and the tightly rolled poncho and front line panels which hung from my belt became twisted across my buttock so that I could not fasten the belt and I cursed fretfully until someone straightened them out. I checked my gear carefully: canteen tops tightly screwed, yes; grenade pins bent sufficiently to keep them from being pulled accidentally but not enough to hamper my pulling them when I needed to, yes; chamber and operating rod of my rifle free of dust, yes; oil and thong case and combination tool in my rifle butt. And my personal possessions; the extra socks were in the hip pocket with my handkerchief; my billfold was in the other hip pocket; my pocket knives were there; the waterproof envelope in which I carried the pictures of my family was secure; my fountain pen was clipped fast in my breast pocket; the extra cigarettes were in the gas mask carrier. I slipped the weather cover over my rifle again, picked it up and went through the hatch, climbed the ladder to the top deck and the railing caught at my bayonet and combat knife and the blackout curtain at the top clutched the gas mask which I had hung like a haversack across my shoulders so that I had to almost stoop to my knees and jerk savagely to free myself and the sudden release plunged me headlong onto the deck. I was angry and afraid that I was showing my nervousness and I felt that I wore too much gear and I wondered how the BAR-man could maneuver at all with his heavier automatic weapon and his larger supply of ammunition.

A line had formed before the starboard bow hatch leading down to the tank deck and I walked to the rear of it across a precarious path of timber-steadied mortar and small arms ammunition boxes made wet and slippery by spray and an early morning mist or dew. I used my rifle as a cane to steady myself and Seiden, standing near the hatch, grinned at me and I smiled in return.

The line moved slowly and I knew that it would be after seven-fifteen before I could get below, but the motion of the men was inexorable and I went down the first ladder to a forward troop compartment and lowered myself through the deck, while a member of the crew held my rifle, to a vertical ladder leading onto the tank deck scarcely more than six feet below. My rifle was passed down, another man began the descent, and I climbed atop the first amphibious tractor and walked along its gunwale to the second, jumping from one to another until I arrived at my tank bearing the twin sign, 5-2, meaning second tank in the fifth wave. I wondered why even today I should feel nettled in my copy reader's mind by its name which was Geronomo and I said someone just went o-happy when he painted it on, but I wished that it could have been corrected.

More than half the men scheduled to ride in the tank already were in it when I entered and they sat, most of them, on the cans of 60-millimeter mortar ammunition, the boxes of machine gun ammunition, and the water cans which we must unload when we hit the beach. But Boudrie the platoon guide and R—— the cook stood at the rear leaning against the ramp, Boudrie

30

holding his rifle in his right hand and R—— clutching a Tommy-gun between his knees. Zeke Koon, the corporal, looking young in his large helmet, stood at the front of the amphibious tractor with Seiden. They were to man the two light machine guns which they were ordered not to fire, for in a previous landing troops in the first wave had been fired upon by overzealous gunners in tanks. The guns were to be used only in case of dire emergency. Sand bags were piled along the gunwales adjacent to the guns and a tank crewman leaned against the bags on the starboard side, looking like something out of the future with his close-fitting helmet, his chin microphone and his brilliant yellow life jacket, now deflated.

Suddenly we were all there, the twenty of us. There were the thirteen members of our squad, the platoon guide, four members of what the operational directive had called platoon headquarters, the demolition sergeant, and Doc Scala, the corpsman.

Groppenbacher, the demolitions sergeant, moved to my left and sat beside me on a mortar ammunition can. He grinned at me, gripped my knee and said:

"Well, pop, what do you think of the war?"

"It's all right, so far," I replied, but the motors of the tanks started and my reply was drowned out. Matchunis, the runner, sat in front of me on a water can and held my rifle while I checked once more on my life belt.

R—— the cook punched me and pointed toward the bow. I stood up and saw that the bow doors were opened, the ramp lowered, and as I watched, the first of the tanks beedled forward, strained heavily up the sharp incline to the ramp and then plunged careening into the water. It bobbled there in front of the ship for a few seconds and then moved slowly off to the starboard, its treads throwing up twin geysers of spray at its stern.

The roar of our motors increased, the treads screeched against the steel deck, and we jerked forward a few feet, swerved awkwardly to the center of the tank deck and moved toward the bow doors and the fumes of the tanks preceding us brought tears into our eyes and made us cough despite the near-gale of air which was pumped through the compartment. Each of us held to the side of the tractor or to someone who held to the side of the tractor for support, and the huge machine thrust its nose into the air suddenly, climbed laboriously, leveled off momentarily, and then plunged sickeningly into the water, scattering the ammunition and water cans under our feet while we clung mightily to our grips, our feet thrust from beneath us. The spray flew back over us, but we did not know it until the tank righted in the water, rolled heavily, then gently, and our treads churned at the water and we too moved to the starboard.

The ship's crew lined the railing of the bow above us and waved at us as we moved slowly away and someone in the tank became for me a gesture rather than a personality when he gave the V-for-victory salute, then curled his forefinger down into the palm of his hand and thrust the other finger into the air. With this defiant and indelicate gesture I realized that the tension was broken for me and I sat back on the mortar can.

The invasion had begun for our company.

4

The tank dipped and fell off in the troughs of the sea and our motors idled and we still swapped grins and gestures with the ship's crew while we waited for the other tanks to emerge from the vessel.

The sun was high in the heaven and all the chill was gone from the air and everyone seemed more relaxed. I stood up and saw off to the starboard the Higgins boat which was the command craft for our wave. And from it Bob Warren, the Coast Guard combat photographer, saw me and waved and nudged the goateed Vic Heyden, the combat correspondent, at his side and Vic also grinned at me and I thought this is better than the last time we saw each other when I felt you were holding a premature wake over me.

The Higgins boat swept by and our own motors roared and we turned to follow it and Boudrie said everybody get down. I sat on the mortar shell container again and saw that although my head was well below the top of the gunwale it was above the water line as defined by the painted mark inside the tank but I was comfortable and did not change my position.

Matchunis—how did he seem always to know everything that was going on? —rummaged in the bottom of the tank and sat up again with a manila-wrapped package in his hand. He unrolled the paper and displayed three sandwiches, one of which he offered to me. I refused.

"I'm about to starve to death," he said, "and I ate a hell of a chow. I don't know what's the matter with me."

I thought he was being ostentatious—*I* didn't feel as if I'd ever want to eat again—but he took a tremendous bite of one of the sandwiches, shifted the mouthful quidlike to his jaw and munched happily.

"My father," he said, "told me never to try to work on an empty stomach."

We new men grinned as we watched him, but the veterans, those who had fought in the Marshalls and on Saipan and Tinian, paid no attention to him.

Beeson, his helmet somehow accentuating the Indianlike high cheek bones and tight-lipped face, stared stolidly before him toward the bow of the tank. In front of him, but facing half center, Hopper, the corporal and my group leader, looked intently at the deck while Turlo, near the bow, twisted his head nervously from side to side, making certain that everything and everyone was in his place. Turlo was standing, but he stooped when Boudrie repeated his order for everyone to keep his head down. Boudrie himself continued to stand.

And then I realized that we new men were lucky for I knew that the veterans already were under fire: the more fortunate were under fire in the Marshalls or on Tinian but most of them were being attacked by the Japanese on Saipan where they had had their most terrible previous ordeal. We new ones, too, had only our minds but our minds now were invincible and immortal and indestructible and although we said to ourselves this may be terrible we accentuated to ourselves only the probability. What we really meant was that it might be awesome and exhausting, but never for an instant did we admit the situation could be serious to the point of being fatal.

Of course we knew that fatalities might and probably would occur but in our mind's eye we saw ourselves as grieving over the loss of friends, for never could we picture our friends grieving over us. Thus does ignorance protect the sanity of the untutored mind.

The tank roared on, for we had reached the LD (line of departure of each wave on its way to the beach), and the noise of the tank was everything; because the ordinary human sounds were replaced by the motor's activity and the battle before us had yet no sound.

We hung three ponchos over the ramp of the tank to trail and become soaked in the sea for our air observers had seen what appeared to be a long row of oil drums buried in the sand of the beach and they had said *those drums may hold explosives or they may hold fuel to blaze up and hold you on the beach under the merciless fire of the enemy mortars or they may be, like those planned by the British in their invasion-fearing days, connected by pipes to the sea and burning oil may be released onto the surface of the water as your tanks come in. But don't worry,* they said; *don't worry for we have tested it out with live goats and we have found that they can ride through blazing water in these tanks without being scorched. Just take these ponchos,* they said, *and wet them to put over the top of your tank and you'll be all right* and I wondered then which goats had dipped *their* ponchos into the water.

But we held the ponchos over the ramp and let them trail in the sea and off our stern perhaps two hundred yards away the sea spouted upward but I heard no sound of the shell which had fallen. We put the ponchos on the deck and forgot about them for Boudrie nudged me and shouted in my ear:

"Some tanks are on the beach!"

I stood again and looked and I saw that they were indeed and it appeared to me that they had even succeeded in scaling the first terrace which lay close to the water's edge. But I wasn't certain and before I could determine if this were so Turlo motioned for me to get down and I sat on my mortar case again.

"Don't you think we ought to load now, Turlo?" Boudrie yelled. Turlo failed to hear but, in a matter of seconds, he shouted:

"Everybody lock and load!"

We peeled the covers off our weapons and I took a clip of ammunition from the side of my cartridge belt, tapped the black-tipped projectile ends on my rifle butt to make certain the bullets were aligned evenly in the clip, stripped back the operating rod handle, pressed the clip down on the follower and slide, and smashed the bolt home with a blow on the operating rod handle from the heel of my palm. I clicked on the safety and placed the rifle, butt down, between my knees, the muzzle pointing directly into the air. But the man with the Tommy-gun cradled his weapon in his arms and the muzzle pointed directly at my head until I put up my hand and forced it around and he grinned apologetically and shifted it so that it pointed into the air.

I realized that Boudrie was shouting and waving and I saw that the tank on our right, the tank which carried the company commander and our platoon leader and Summers' squad had moved in until its radio antenna bobbed only a few feet beyond and above our starboard gunwale.

"Get that damn thing away from here, get it away! Do you want to draw their fire out here?"

No one in the other tractor could hear him, of course, but the antenna moved off to the right and it was impossible to tell whether that tank or our own had shifted its position.

The tank crewman left his post near the machine gun and worked his way quickly to the port side aft near the ramp and Turlo stood up and shouted:

"Everybody take something! Everybody take something! We've got to get this stuff on the beach!"

The ramp controls ground in my ear and at the same time we bumped solidly. We had hit ground. The tank motors slowed momentarily then roared again and once more idled and the ramp crashed and I saw without thinking that it led into the water at the rear and we hadn't been able to go over that terrace.

I turned to my right and grabbed the first thing I saw, which was a five-gallon can of drinking water, and someone started down the ramp treads on the right of me and another person ran down the treads on the left and I moved down the center which was treadless and already wet from the surf and my feet skidded from under me and I fell half sitting in the shallow water. But almost before I had fallen someone seized me under the right armpit and hauled me to my feet and my rifle was dry because I had almost by instinct held it above my head when I started to slide.

The roar of the tank was gone. In its place there was another roar which was different, for where the sound of the tank was a one-ness this was a conglomeration of all the noises ever heard but I didn't hear it until minutes or perhaps an hour later, for hearing and comprehension require thought and my mind only said to me all the lessons which it had received about the attack. It said, *run run run get off the beach get off the beach don't ever hole up on the beach unless it's absolutely necessary because they are sighting in on the beach and they'll get you sure as hell get off the beach put this damn thing down and get off the beach and run.*

But I couldn't run because of the weight of the gear and of the water can and because the sand into which I sank up to my calves so that every step was a conscious uprooting of my feet and placing them one in front of the other and my weight seemed to grow (it had, from the sand clinging to my wet feet and legs) and I said to myself *run* but I only shuffled and staggered and something compelled me to look back to my right (I don't remember any sound but it must have been there) and the beach sand spouted up like black water from a geyser. I knew that a shell had fallen close by but it meant nothing to me because I had not been hit.

Then I saw someone in front of me drop the ammunition which he carried and I released my grip on the water can; I must have run no more than ten yards onto the beach from the water's edge. I moved faster when I had abandoned the can but only for a few steps; I realized that already I was tired. I was possessed with a compelling desire for a drink of water, for my mouth was so dry that gum which I had been chewing suddenly adhered to my teeth and to my gums and to my tongue and to my lips when I tried to spew it forth.

It glued itself to every surface it touched and hung in maddening threads within the cavity of my mouth. With my tongue I worked most of the substance to my lips where it stuck until I bit it off and let it fall to the ground; tiny bits of it hung from my lips to my chin. All this happened as I ran and shuffled and stumbled and the telling of it requires more time than it occupied me on the beach, which was only a matter of a few steps.

Later that day I thought of the words which I had read picturing such an attack and to me the honesty of them had fled. I knew then that the writers had seen too much. But perhaps their heads were clearer than mine and perhaps they had not been obsessed with the idea of *get off the beach get inland don't stop now run run run*. Possibly I had been remiss, not they.

For although I had wanted desperately to form a picture of what it was like to be on a beach under fire, all that came through was the recollection of my mental prodding and a few scenes, disconnected in time and space, some of them faded as with age and out of focus, and only one or two sharp and clear.

What I saw were dozens of figures running and stumbling aimlessly about me and they had to me neither faces nor uniforms nor weapons. They were merely forms which moved under some strange compulsion and were charged by emotions which I could never fathom. Perhaps no emotion existed and all the action was instinctive. But that could not be correct, for instinct would have driven us back, not forward; it is with the annihilation of such that training is concerned and it must have succeeded, for although forms floated in front of me and alongside me none of them was going toward the rear.

But there was another picture which is as vivid to

39

me now as it was then and with it is related the only clear sound which I distinguished on the beach that morning. For as I ran toward the first terrace I heard to my left the cry:

"Co-o-o-rpsman! Co-o-o-rpsman! Oh co-o-o-rps-man!"

It was a shout without being a shout; it was a wail which denied all the training of the trooper for in it was everything primal: fear, pain, and agonized terror. It was a wail without an end or a beginning but somehow it was repeated and how I heard it over the furious sound of the beach I'll never know but I did.

I looked to the left and in a shallow hole against the terrace I saw the man sitting on his left hip, his legs sprawling lifelessly sideward. He was leaning on his left hand, and his head was turned back and to the side and his mouth was open. I saw no motion of mouth or face or wide staring eyes but I knew it was from that mouth that those sounds issued. It was like a picture painted and hung against a gallery wall and in that instant I knew its every detail as if I had studied it for months.

To his left lay three Marines and I knew they were dead more certainly than if I had examined their pulses or listened to their breathing, for they were heaped in the peculiar positions which death uses to distinguish its victims from the unconscious. Death is not merely content to rob of life; it must take dignity, too. Even the one man who lay curled on his side did not preserve the illusion of sleep; his head was turned sharply to the left and his face was thrust into the sand. The second lay spread eagled on his face with his hands and feet flung far apart as if they had been nailed there. The third was on his knees with his feet apart and his toes pointing inward toward each other and the weight of his upper body rested on the side of his head and his shoulders; arms were extended flat along the ground beside his legs. The picture was so clear that I saw the tightness of his trousers across his rump and the bulge of some object in his left hip pocket and I saw that one canteen had twisted to the left so that it hung almost touching the ground while the other lay in the middle of his back and his poncho tucked in his cartridge belt was unfolded along the left side of his back. His helmet was not on his head.

I hurled myself against the terrace and my breath came in shallow wheezing gasps. I lay there and panted for what seemed hours but must have been only seconds grown fat and indolent.

And my mental prodding to *get off the beach get off the beach* refused to recognize my physical anguish and I arose to a crouch and tried to sprint up the terrace wall but my feet only bogged in the sand and instead of running I crawled, trying to keep my rifle clean but failing. At the top of the wall I pulled to my feet and saw directly in front of me a shell hole with another slightly farther inland to the left and I decided to run to the second but by the time I had passed the first my run again had become a walk and I said to myself I am a fine target standing upright here and I strained to run again but I succeeded only in falling down and so weak was I that instead of crawling I could only roll. I rolled until I was over the edge of the hole and into safety.

I sat up on the side of the hole near the bottom and my mouth was so dry that the roof hurt when I ran my tongue over it. I swallowed to try to renew the flow of saliva but the only thing which I swallowed was my palate which seemed to have grown inches. I retched violently and the saliva began to flow so I swallowed again, retched again, and felt better.

Six men were in the hole with me, but it could have accommodated many more. (I was thankful that it did not; we had been acidly instructed in the dangers, tactical and personal, of troops' bunching together even in refuge.) The first person I recognized was young Horton who had come over from the States with me. He sat on the bottom of the crater, holding his rifle in his hand while Doc Scala, the corpsman for our platoon, bandaged his left hand. Horton and I stared owlishly at each other, unsmiling and apathetic as if we had never seen each other before. Then he held his rifle up and showed me a long gash in the upper hand guard where a missile had struck and he shrugged as if to say that was a close call, wasn't it?

"Did it get you anywhere else?" I asked, for his motion had broken the hypnotic trance which seemed to possess me.

He shook his head.

"How about you?" I asked the short, thick-set boy who lay beside him, his arm and his leg already bandaged.

"I think I'm hit bad," he said and he was frightened. "I've got it in the stomach, too."

He opened his khaki shirt and showed me the hole, about half the size of a pencil's diameter above his belt. It was not yet bandaged, and it did not bleed. The edges were puffed and white. I shook my head and wanted to say something encouraging or to do something but I could do neither except to advise, "Take it easy."

And I saw Rice, a BAR-man in my squad, across the

42

crater, breathing heavily and crouched against the side near the top. I shook my head and said:

"I'm pooped."

"I am, too. I'm so exhausted I can't move. I'm going to have to stay here awhile."

But again the urgency of my need for motion gripped me and I scrambled up the side of the pit near Rice, stopped for a moment until my breathing eased, and moved again into the open, crouching low and running with an easier stride. But when I fell into the next shell hole again my mouth was tortured by its dryness and my breath whistled through my mouth and the blood pumped so that I could feel my temples expand and contract within the fatigue cap which I wore under my helmet.

This time, I lay longer and for the first time I opened my canteen, the snaps of which were so fouled with sand that I thought I should have to rip them off in my compelling desire for a drink. For I had swallowed and retched again but the saliva had refused to flow and I continued to retch in spite of myself now and I was afraid that if I didn't drink I should vomit. I drank and the water felt foreign and cool within my mouth but it did not comfort my mouth as the saliva had done before. So I lay on my side on the bank of the crater and rested.

A boy whose face was familiar but whose name I did not know said:

"I see Middleditch got it."

"No! Bad?"

"I don't think too bad. Hit in the foot, I think. I saw him lying back there and he didn't seem to be hurt too bad."

And I wondered if anyone had picked up his Browning automatic rifle, for we had been told in training that firepower was the vital thing in the attack and that if a BAR-man were hit the man nearest him should pick up his BAR and ammunition belt, sacrificing his own weapon if it had less firepower. And our instructor, emphasizing the need, had said if this platoon is cut down until it has only nine men, I want all nine of them to be BAR-men.

For the first time since I had left the terrace wall I examined my own weapon and I saw that sand lay thick along the operating rod groove and I took out my cleaning brush and dusted it thoroughly. But when I tried to open the bolt the operating rod handle would not move and I finally had to kick it open. I removed the clip and worked with my brush at the rod, the locking lugs, and grooves. I oiled the parts thoroughly and tested the rifle with my hand and the bolt moved smoothly again, so I re-inserted the clip and shot the bolt home. I wished I had something to wrap about the operating rod handle to keep the dust out and I looked for my rifle cover but couldn't find it and I recalled that I must have dropped it on the deck of the tank when I had loaded my rifle while coming into the beach.

Rested again, I moved around the inside of the crater and looked cautiously over the side. I saw men ahead and to the side of me pop out of and into the ground and this time the motions were jerky and intensely human and not, as on the beach, fantastically other-worldly. The timing of the entire scene was uneven so that at one instant and in one area I could see a host of men struggling forward, and then none when all disappeared under cover, and then a trickle as they began to venture forth. The figures moved with a frantic awkwardness, crouched until their bodies were almost parallel to the ground, and their dust-raising strides looked as mine had felt: almost unbearably difficult to execute. Some, more heavily burdened or more fatigued or, perhaps in some cases, more indifferent to the danger, strode heavily and without apparent haste. I saw no one I recognized beyond my crater for the sameness of the deep helmets and the gray-green battle dress bred anonymity. Then for the first time since I had left I thought of the beach and for the first time also I really heard its sounds, the thousand sounds which made up its one noise, the screams and hisses and cracklings and even, somewhere back there, a shouting voice. Already the drumming of the barrage was so incessant that it had built up in my consciousness a tonal pattern like the background music of a movie, really heard only when it was broken by the dissonance of a close hit or the nearby passage of shell fragments or small arms projectiles.

But always was I conscious of the sand. The terrain about me looked like an unbroken sea of it, a sea which could wash over me and cover me. Already it had filtered like water through my clothing and into my eyes and nose, and my teeth had a fine grittiness to them which could not be wiped off with my tongue.

Again I looked forward, this time hunting for someone from my squad, for Rice had been the only member I had seen since I left the tank. I saw no one I recognized and I sprinted forward to another hole. It was empty.

I fumbled for my canteen again and swished the water inside my mouth for several seconds before I swallowed. This time it tasted better than it had before and I thought I'd better be careful; I'll drink all my water and there won't be a chance to get any more.

And I remembered how I had told Turlo that I needed very little water and he said, "Well, you stick around me in combat; I'll drink all you don't use. Boy, I get thirsty!"

And suddenly Turlo was there with me, half running, half crawling from the direction of the front.

"You seen any of the rest of the guys?" he panted.

"I saw Rice back there in a shell hole. He said he was tired out and couldn't move up then, but he'll be along. Have you seen any?"

"Beeson and Kennedy, they're over there." He motioned to the right. "And West is up there."

"Chico," he said abruptly, "has been hit."

"Oh God. Bad? Where?"

"Yeh, pretty bad." My expression must have been strange for he said hastily: "Oh, I think he'll be all right. But his shoulder is pretty badly shot up."

"Middleditch got it, too."

"Middleditch? You sure? You see him?"

"No, but somebody down there told me he saw him. Shot through the foot, he said. Said he didn't seem to be too badly hurt."

"Say, Matchu," it was almost like an afterthought, "look at my shoulder. I think I'm hit. I can't be sure, but it feels numb."

For the first time I noticed a fleck of blood across his temple and I looked at his right shoulder. There was a small snagged hole in his dungaree jacket at the rear.

"Yeh, I'm afraid so. There's a hole here. Oh God, here's another here," and I showed him a larger torn place, evidently caused by a small shell fragment, in the front of the same shoulder. "Why don't you go back and get it treated?"

"No, I'll be all right. It's just numb and a little stiff."

Sand flowed down the side of the crater and Captain Harshbarger, the company commander, slid over the edge into the bottom, followed closely by Krakovitz, in camp one of the two company musics, but out here the captain's runner. The captain smiled.

"Oh, hello there. All right?"

"Yessir. Fine. But I think Turlo has been wounded."

The captain looked concerned.

"Here, you'd better let me look at that. Take off some of that gear and loosen your jacket."

I helped Turlo remove his gear. The wound in front was only a scratch, but the skin at the rear of his shoulder was punctured and it was obvious that shrapnel was imbedded in his flesh. The flow of blood evidently had been small but it had stopped and only a round stain on his undershirt showed that he had bled at all. The captain tore open a first aid packet, ripped a hole in the corner of an envelope containing sulfanilamide and sprinkled the medication over the wound.

"There," he said, "I think that'll be all right. That's about all a corpsman could do for you except to put on a battle dressing and I don't think that's necessary since the bleeding already has stopped."

Turlo replaced his jacket and we sat in silence for a few minutes. Other men came into the hole, some walking, some running, but all breathing as if they'd run great distances. Their shoes and trouser legs were caked with sand but their faces still were clean, yet so stiffened by strain that they looked like masks, making it difficult to recognize even some members of my own company. Almost to a man they carried their rifles in their right hands, the weapons parallel to the ground with the loosened gun slings forming round loops toward the earth. They were usually silent as they entered and gave no sign of recognition. They sat heavily along the sides of the crater, some leaning their heads against their hands which clasped the weapons placed butt-downward on the sand. And some lay back against the walls of the crater, staring silently at nothing in the sky. All talked little, and then only when they had regained their breath or had lighted cigarettes.

But one fell as soon as he reached the bottom of the pit and he lay on his side, his head cradled in his forearms, his fingers clutched together behind his head.

"He hit?"

"No. Concussion. He can't hear."

"I think he'd better go back if he can't hear," the captain said. "He'll need some medical attention."

The man lay without moving, his eyes closed, his face contorted, and I thought that's another one gone; he'll never be able to go on. (I was wrong. I saw him four days later, his hearing restored, and he apparently had suffered no other ill effects from the blast.)

The captain looked at his watch and then peered forward out of the hole.

"I'd better move on," he said and with the words he ran out of the crater.

"Do you want me along?" Krakovitz shouted after him.

"You bet!" The captain already was well away from the hole so that his words were almost lost and someone repeated them to Krakovitz who picked up his carbine and followed the officer.

Turlo also made preparations to go forward again.

"Where's the squad? What do you want me to do—come with you?" I asked.

"You wait here. I'm just going up to the next hole. It's already pretty crowded. Wait here until you see me move out again and then follow me."

He inched cautiously out of the shelter and then broke into a low, awkward run until he disappeared. I moved to where he had been and I could see him lying with two other men in a shallow hole behind a tiny hillock several yards away.

I looked back to find that two others from company headquarters had come into the hole: First Sergeant Pollock and Gunnery Sergeant Lewis. Lewis looked as unperturbed as I had heard he was under fire and he settled back comfortably and lighted a cigarette. Then he grinned at me.

"How's it coming, old man? What do you think of the war?"

"I don't know much about it yet, but as far as I can see it's hell."

"You ain't just shitting." He turned to the first sergeant. "By God, this morning I felt worse—more nervous—about this one than I've ever felt before. It got me down." His apparent coolness made his words sound like a joke.

"Oh Godamighty! I wish I was back in Dago with my foot on the rail blowing the suds off a glass of beer," he said.

"And I wish I were back there holding your hand," I said.

"I guess this makes the newspaper business look pretty good, doesn't it?"

"You're damn right. I intended to spend the next war behind a desk, too."

"Where's your squad, Matthews?" the first sergeant asked.

"Right up there."

"Why aren't you with them?"

"Turlo told me to stay here until he moved out and then to follow him."

"Is he still there?"

I looked over the edge of the hole.

"Yes."

He subsided and I lighted a cigarette. We settled back and rested until someone shouted:

"By God, the tanks are ashore. Here they come."

We looked out of the hole. Six of the vehicles moved like huge camouflaged bugs in a line toward the front. They were about a hundred yards to our right and almost abreast of us when they stopped. A cloud of sand, black with smoke, spewed out of the ground a few yards in front of the first tank and seconds later another shell hit to the rear and closer. The tanks made no effort to move.

"By God, are they going to let the f——g things sit there until the artillery gets them?" the gunnery sergeant asked angrily.

And the ground about us rocked and rolled and the air turned black and flamed and the sand cascaded down the sides of our crater and we clung to the ground but of course then it was too late for the shell had struck and the shrapnel had shrilled off. We had heard nothing but the flashing crack of the explosion which blotted out the sound of the flying fragments.

None of us was hurt but we were shaken and we looked at each other first in wonder and then we grinned self-consciously as if to say that one almost had our number. The gunnery sergeant said:

"God damn those tanks, anyway. They're going to sit there until they get the shit kicked out of them and out of us, too."

He shook his head in wonder.

"This is the hottest beach *I* ever saw."

"You mean it's worse than Saipan?" I asked.

"I think so. Don't you, top?"

The first sergeant said nothing but he also shook his head in bewilderment.

"Yeh, I think it is," the gunnery sergeant continued. "In this way, I mean. The shelling may have been as bad on Saipan, but there we were able to get off the beach and under cover. The beach was narrow and there were trees and jungle we could get into. But here everything is beach and you just can't get off it and there's damn little cover."

As he talked the dead dull whacks of the exploding mortar shells and the sharper cracks of the bursting artillery shells continued, followed by the whining and burbling of the flying fragments. When the shells fell at a distance you could hear almost all their sounds of life except their discharge from the weapons. You could hear, when they came thus, the sizzling which sounded like chicken frying in deep fat followed by the crash of the explosion. But when they dropped nearer you heard less—only the deadly sibilant, like a sharply drawn sigh or like a gentle breeze in a leafy tree, before the bedlam of contact. When they dropped on top of you you heard nothing but the roaring crash and the ground heaved beneath you. When the shrapnel was small it whined like an angry bee, sometimes merely for the briefest of moments, sometimes for seconds which seemed like minutes, as if the fragment were circling your head trying to make up its mind whether

51

to strike you now or later and when this happened you instinctively flattened yourself against the ground.

Our muscles ached from the tension of our bodies against the whining that grew in intensity and in frequency as the tanks maintained their positions near us. We shrank into ourselves when the whining was replaced by the loud tailless crashed when the shells overshot their mark and fell near us and we cursed the day that tanks were invented. Our anger was irrational, for the tanks were fashioned for a certain type of warfare, and this was not that type. They needed, for instance, the protective cover of superior fire power either from our big guns or our planes. Under what might have been only temporarily superior enemy fire power—and now, certainly, the Japanese heavy weapons could assert themselves almost at will on almost any point of the island—they were as defenseless as the foot soldiers were.

The tanks were at another disadvantage. The threat of land mines caused them to rely almost completely on the ability of walking demolitions men to clear paths for them, and now under the merciless artillery, mortar, and machine gun fire all our foot troops were tied down, and that meant that the tanks were, too.

Our company had landed near the extreme right of the beachhead and the tanks had worked their way even farther to our right under the cliffs which abruptly terminated the beach. Thus the tanks, like the infantrymen, were subjected to violent, plunging, flat trajectory artillery fire as well as to the mortar fire. Unlike the troops, however, they made a startling target against the sand.

The island was so small, too, that maneuvering, the

essence of a tank's life, was entirely out of the question. The vehicles were faced not only by obstacles which the enemy had erected but by those created by our own bombing and shellfire which had pitted the face of the island as if it had suffered from a mighty pox. Where the huge craters were the salvation of the infantryman—they were his only cover—they were the death of the tanks.

For as we cowered in our shell hole the artillery fire advanced on us and retreated, advanced and retreated, trying to pattern out the positions of the tanks. And then came a crash and roar which flattened us against the sides of our pit and on its heels another roar so that when the whine of the shrapnel passed, showing the blast had not been too close, we looked up and thick black smoke as solid as a rock column raised itself to our right.

"They've gotten a tank," someone shouted. And we looked over the rim of the crater.

It was true; the smoke issued from the top of the tank where the turret had been, for it was there no longer. Lazy flames, looking small under the huge and growing pile of smoke, licked from inside the steel. And more shells fell in the area.

We fidgeted nervously inside our hole for we knew our position was getting too hot for us. But rather than jam other holes in the vicinity we stayed where we were.

Then I heard the first sergeant's voice:

"They're moving out ahead."

I looked up in time to see Turlo's back, hunched over as he crouched, moving forward, and I crawled to the forward edge of our crater and lay on my side, awaiting the fall of the next shell.

53

It fell. I pressed my face and my body into the sand and then gathered my legs under me.

The gunnery sergeant grinned at me, waved his hand and said:

"Okay, now, pop. Take it easy."

I pushed my way into the clear and broke into a run.

5

I could see nothing of Turlo. Directly in front of me was the hole from which he had dashed and I ran into it and flung myself on my belly.

Two other men were there yet and when I recovered my breath and my powers of observation I realized that I was lying at the heels of Gene Alderman. Alderman was one of the men who had greeted me when I first joined the Fourth Division; the others had been on maneuvers. At that time he had been assigned to the rear echelon, one of a group of men thought above the age for combat, or physically unfit, to be left behind to care for the base when the troops sailed for the next operation.

But Alderman had resented his age classification and, although we wrote his wife that he was safe from the dangers of combat, he continued to ask for reclassification. Only a few days before we boarded ship he was assigned to our platoon. He had never disclosed his change in status to his wife and she, when she read of the division's landing, must have believed him still safe on the island of Maui.

We spoke a few words, asking each other about the safety of friends and alternately cringing beneath the bursts of enemy fire and cursing the shallowness of our hole. The third man, whose appearance was only vaguely familiar, lay at an angle in front of Alderman, propped on his elbows with his rifle held before him. His face which he turned toward us was long and gray with fatigue and he beat out the tempo of the enemy barrage as he automatically ducked his head and jerked up his arms into a protective cradle each time a shell burst. In a short time, however, he moved out into the open and Alderman and I wormed our way forward in the hole. Alderman crouched for a moment on his elbows and knees then broke into a low sprint and I took over his position at the front of the hole.

The whining and the cracking of the shellfire increased and I lay flat but when it slackened I rose to my knees, looked quickly about to try to locate my squad, ducked without reason and then scrambled to my feet again.

I headed out toward my direct front. My eye glimpsed two holes either of which could serve as the next possible haven. Lying on the rim of the one immediately ahead of me, his leg drawn up as if he were preparing to push himself up for the next dash, lay a Marine. I knew he was dead and I veered immediately to the left and entered the second crater.

Five men sat there and they waved me deeper into the pit. One of them said:

"I guess you know Miley was hit?"

"Nap?"

"Uh-huh."

"Where?"

"Leg."

"Bad?"

"I don't think so. I think it was through the fleshy part of the leg. Anyhow, I saw him walking back with Heidorn."

"Heidorn? He hit, too?"

"Yeh; through the foot."

"Seen anybody else from the first squad?"

"Beeson's in your squad, isn't he?"

"Yeh."

"He's around somewhere. I saw him a few minutes ago."

"Was he all right?"

"Oh, yeh. He was moving forward just ahead of here the last time I saw him."

"Guess I'd better shove along, too. Take it easy," and I moved around behind the men's shoulders and peered over the lip of the hole to determine the next avenue of advance.

A small hole lay to the left about 20 yards but I could see the helmets of other men already there. To my direct front was a large crater, and although it appeared about 50 yards away, an inordinately long distance, I decided to run for it.

My leggings and my trousers from the knees to the ankles had dried and I lay back and beat the caked sand off them as best I could for I realized that the added weight of the sand might have accounted for some of my earlier exhaustion. At the same time I unrolled my trousers legs which I had turned up, cuff-like, on the outside of my leggings and more sand cascaded to the ground.

I rolled over to my stomach, lifted myself to my hands and knees and crawled to the top of the crater and then bolted to the direct front.

But I veered quickly to my left and something grabbed at my stomach and lungs and squeezed them so that I almost gasped for breath. To my right and barely five yards away rose, almost a foot out of the ground, the square walls of a Japanese concrete pillbox. But even as the lightning instinct of my fear turned me to the left, I veered to the right again, for I saw that from two apertures in the thick walls smoke was coming and my fright left me.

But as I ran I cursed my stupidity and my eyesight for I knew that unless I were more careful the next time it might be rifle or machine gun fire issuing from those ports, not smoke. This pillbox had been wiped out by the men ahead of me, but some would inevitably be by-passed and it would take only the overlooking of one to be the end for me. How had I missed this one anyhow? It was not well camouflaged. It was small—probably three feet square along the top—but it sat upright above the sand, its lines undisguised. But I had looked past it in the glance I took for my next haven and I knew I was lucky to be alive. And I thought these thoughts as I ran.

Even as the fright had struck me, it was replaced by a reaction almost of hilarity. I neared the shell hole and on the opposite side I saw Ray Marine, with whom I had spent part of last night (was it only last night?). And as I ran I grinned at him and he grinned back and I raced to the edge of the hole and leaped well into it, yelling:

"Make way for the old man."

But as I landed my feet poured sand over the shoulders of a man I hadn't seen and on his rifle. Before he turned his head he said violently:

"God *damn* you! Be careful!"

I saw that he held a cleaning brush in his hand and had been working on his rifle and I had undone his work.

I apologized and he turned around. It was John Hartman, Marine's tentmate and a friend of mine. His scowl vanished when he saw me but his voice still had a tinge of angriness when he said:

"Hi, pop. How're you doing?"

"I'm sorry I fouled up your rifle, Baby," I said, "but I'd a lot rather foul up your rifle than come in slower and have the Japs foul me up."

"I guess you're right there," he said and he went to work again with his brush on the operating rod groove which was filled with dirt.

I took out my brush and dug at my weapon also, for, without the cascade of sand which had swept over Hartman's, there was very little difference in the appearance of the two rifles.

I still sat above and behind Hartman. Below and in front of me about ten men were grouped. The hole was tremendous and it was connected to my left with what appeared to be another of about the same size. The edges of the two overlapped so that a recess about two feet deep joined them.

As I sat there, a blond boy directly across the hole from me cried sharply and pressed his hand to the right side of his face which was turned to me, and blood spurted and then oozed between his fingers.

I don't remember anyone's calling for a corpsman but almost immediately one was there. It was again Doc Scala from our platoon and he bent over the wounded man. I realized that the injury must have been inflicted by a missile which came over or near my head and I worked my way lower into the hole.

The wounded man was silent after the first outcry and the others of us in the hole were silent, too. Perhaps it was for most, as it was for me, the first time they had been with a man when he was wounded although all of us had seen many dead and wounded since we had come ashore.

My hilarity, which had not been deflated entirely by the tongue-lashing I had received from Hartman, was gone now. But as I watched the corpsman I was aware of someone to my left standing bolt upright. The very idea was so preposterous I almost ignored it until I realized this figure was motioning to me.

I looked and the man, his rifle slung over his shoulder, leveled a miniature camera at me, clicked the shutter, smiled, waved, and sank below the level of the adjoining ground. I was spellbound.

And while I watched, the same figure arose, slowly, and carefully got his focus and snapped again.

It was Frank Degliequi, a corporal in another squad of my platoon. He was the first man from my organization I'd seen since Turlo and Alderman had left me in the shallow shell hole. I crawled over near the depression joining the two craters, looked around to exchange a "Take it easy" with Marine, and dived through the space into the spot where I'd seen Degliequi.

This apparently was a temporary headquarters for my platoon. The commander, Lieutenant Verica, was there along with Platoon Sergeant Updegrave, their runners, and several other members of my outfit.

"Has anybody here seen Turlo's squad?" I asked.

"Yes; it's right over there," and Updegrave pointed

60

off to the left front. "Get your breath and then you'd better join the squad. We want to form our lines as soon as possible."

"Who's up there?"

"Oh, Beeson and Kennedy and Turlo and West and a couple of others."

"Has anybody here seen Hopper?"

"I haven't."

"How about Seiden or Laramie or Koon?"

"Don't know where they are."

"I guess you know Middleditch got it?"

"No! We heard about Chico and Miley. Was it bad?"

I told them what I had heard and they told me of others they had known who were hurt or killed and we sat in what was almost stupefaction for it was evident that our company had been hit hard. And I realized that the more we sat and talked of casualties the less appetizing would be the idea of getting out into the open again and before I could hear any more I got to my feet and plunged off in the direction in which Updegrave had pointed.

But when I reached the next hole and found West and Kennedy there I went through the same routine again for they thought of the same things I thought of; the same ideas were the common property of all of us on the island.

Turlo interrupted by vaulting into the hole.

"Get ready to move out."

"Which way?" Kennedy asked.

"Right up there." He pointed to a gully-like trench about 50 yards away to our right front. "Hold up there until you get the word to move on."

"For God's sake let's keep contact," Kennedy implored. "We want to know when to move and when to stop."

"Yeh, we'll have to keep contact, all right. You guys keep your eye on me. I'll be to your right."

He jumped out of the hole and disappeared again and Kennedy and West and I, letting a few seconds elapse, dashed off in a crouching, swerving, scurrying line. It was a long run and each of us was panting heavily as we piled into a huddling heap.

Our cover apparently once had been a communications trench but it had swollen places, like pigs in a python, where shells had distended the walls.

One other man, a stranger to me, occupied the trench when we moved in and soon afterward Beeson slid down beside us. Beeson expressed the belief the trench was overcrowded and after sitting a few minutes started off to join Turlo.

But others continued to filter in by ones and twos and then larger groups. Almost immediately the mortar shells, which had left us alone for the past few minutes, began fingering inquisitively about in our area. We cursed and one man said:

"Well, here we go again. I had me a nice hole down near the beach and not much was happening around me and be God damn if the first platoon didn't move in with me and bring their f——g families. All hell started to cut loose and I cleared out and came up here. Now here comes that God damn first platoon again. . . .

"For Christ's sake, you guys, don't crowd up this place. Get going as soon as possible."

And singly and in small groups between the shell bursts the men moved on but others came in their place, some trailing their squads or platoons or companies and others frankly and fearfully lost.

"You birds know where L Company is?"

"What regiment?"

"Twenty-fifth."

"Yeh. I heard a call going up a few minutes ago for all members of L Company to move to the right. They're moving up on the airport from that direction."

Or:

"Jesus! I don't know where the hell I am. Seen Baker Company?"

"Yeh; they're straight ahead. I think if you'll look right up there you might see some of them."

And the stranger squinted over the edge and ducked back excitedly.

"By God! they're on the edge of the airport!"

We scrambled to our knees and looked to where he pointed. A small cluster of Marines moved cautiously up the terrace leading to the runway. Two inched over onto the level ground and the dust spurted suddenly to their left and they tumbled back to the terrace side and lay there a few seconds before they moved. They then crawled to a point just below the crest of the terrace, halted, and dug feverishly at the bank with their hands.

Other groups, moving rapidly but cautiously, joined them to their left and then to their right and the embankment began to look alive with the gray-green of the Marine dungarees. And we felt that the world was good again and the feeling of invincibility in my mind was strengthened. It was only early afternoon and what I felt surely must be the worst half mile of the island had been traversed in strength. I took another drink of water from my canteen.

The side of the shell hole over my head crumbled

and I looked up to see Seiden sprint by me. He veered, stopped, and sat in front of me, breathing heavily, and grinned.

"Hello."

"Where the hell have you been?"

"I got pinned down back there. I didn't think I was ever going to get up here. But I brought company." He pointed behind me and I turned to see Ray Laramie slide into the crater.

"Zeke was in the hole with us, but he didn't come up the same way we did. I guess he'll be along."

"Did you see Hopper?"

"No."

We were silent a moment.

"How are the rest of them?" he asked. I told him what I knew.

"No one seems to have seen him," someone said. It was an afterthought and we knew he was referring to Hopper. We were worried.

"I heard both Hill and Izell are missing. Nobody has seen them all day." Hill and Izell were almost inseparable friends. Both of them were sergeants and Izell had had a long service overseas. Before he joined the Fourth Division he had been a member of one of the colorful Marine raider battalions.

We talked worriedly, too, of the men who we knew were wounded and we wondered aloud if they had been evacuated safely for we knew, and said so, that it was probably as dangerous for them to go back over the shell-raked beach as it had been for them to cross it after landing. Turlo interrupted our thoughts and our conversation by warning us to stand by to move up. I thrust my canteen back in its cover and buckled the cartridge belt which I had loosened for comfort. I tried

64

my rifle again and again I found the bolt stuck with sand. I worked at it feverishly with the brush and wondered what would happen if I had to use it suddenly. I resigned myself to feeding each round by hand.

We got to our feet and moved irresolutely, uncertain when or in which direction to advance but we heard Turlo shout and saw Beeson run from the hole on our right. One by one we filed out of our crater and moved toward the left front.

Along the route we split and I found myself in a hole with Laramie and Beeson and Kennedy. We had been there only a short while when Koon jumped in with us. Our cover consisted of two holes, one deep and wide in which Laramie and I sat; the other and smaller one adjoined and opened directly into it.

Beeson, Kennedy, and Koon sat in the second hole talking quietly and Laramie and I lay back on the sand and stared at each other. I was tired and said so and he agreed that he was also. We said little and both of us ducked involuntarily whenever we heard the sizzling of shells or the whine of their fragments although I knew by then that the ones you hear are like the lightning you see: they seldom hurt you.

But our time of relaxation was short-lived for the hole began to fill with men, this time from the Twenty-third Marines. They were supposed to be on our left and I wondered whether we or they were out of position.

Evidently the other three men of our squad in the adjoining hole had the same thought, for Kennedy passed at a crouching walk.

"I'm going to find out what the scoop is," he said.

"Let us know what you learn. Do you want us to come with you or to stay here?"

"Stay here. I'll let you know if they want us to move."

He disappeared to the right and Laramie and I lay back. We now were surrounded by men from the Twenty-third and they stretched out carelessly or examined their rifles or curled up tightly frightened and they too were concerned not with their positions or what they were to do next but with their casualties. They named them in ones and twos and they related the tragedies of the day with a kind of horrified relish and their manner showed they considered themselves singularly blessed by Providence. But one or two were merely hungry and they fished in their pockets or gas mask carriers and brought forth cans of C and K rations and large tropical chocolate bars which they sampled and passed around and then finished. I refused an offer of canned beef stew; I wasn't hungry although I had not eaten for nearly twelve hours.

The sun already was slanting low in the west and the part of my body covered by the shadows thrown by the side of the shell hole was chilly. I moved upward along the side of the crater to get more of my body in the sun and then decided that it was safer to be cool and moved back to my original position and buttoned my combat jacket.

Koon and Beeson, tired of waiting for the information on the next move, walked warily out to the right in the direction Kennedy had taken, admonishing Laramie and me to remain where we were until told to move on.

I had started up when they passed but I settled back and, from the cue of a boy in front of me, I unlaced my leggings and removed my shoes, which felt tight on my feet. I upturned one of them and the sand filled my palm and overflowed onto the ground. It evidently had poured in over the tops of my leggings and worked its way down into my shoes. The other shoe was in the same condition and I emptied it onto the ground. My socks still were damp, mostly from the wetting in the sea early in the morning but perhaps partly from sweat and I took them off, shook them thoroughly, turned them inside out and shook them again. My feet were getting cold and I put the socks on and rested my feet on my leggings while I brushed the last of the sand and dust from the inside of my shoes with my fingers. I put my shoes on and the warmth of them felt good but it emphasized the coolness of the rest of my body so that, after I relaced my leggings, I huddled in my combat jacket and tried to coax warmth from it.

The crater appeared to be more and more the property of the outfit from the Twenty-third and newcomers not only filled it but overflowed to the hole to the right and an officer, undistinguishable from the privates about him except for the numeral on his back, tried to bring order out of the chaos.

He took the tiny field radio from his runner and his unsuccessful "Kayo Fox two calling Kayo Fox six— over" set up a pattern of quiet desperation which was only broken when he tried to oust the non-members of his platoon from the hole.

We explained to him that our outfit was nearby to the right and that we had been told to wait orders before moving out. It seemed that we were going to be ejected anyhow when Sergeant Summers, in command of the second squad of our platoon, called and told us the platoon was moving out to the right.

Laramie and I arose immediately. The enemy fire was noticeably lighter now and the most disturbing noise was the sound of a light machine gun which fired in short quick bursts—much more rapid than those from our guns—from our left rear.

Occasionally we saw the quick flicker of a tracer and one of the veterans of previous campaigns against the Japanese was impressed by this remarkable innovation. The enemy, he said, had not previously used tracers for fear of disclosing the positions of their guns. Now, he said, he believed the tracers were being used to point out concentrations of our troops for the benefit of artillery and mortar-observers.

"I've noticed," he said, "that almost every time the machine gun fires often at one target the mortars and artillery begin to sight in on the same place." And I thought then that he must have been keeping his head out of the ground a great deal more than I had been—either that or he was merely trying to make what might be a plausible explanation sound unimpeachable.

But the machine gun fire did not seem to be directed toward our positions and I believed that a slight rise in the ground between us and the airport gave us sufficient protection. We broke into a run, scorning the safety and also the discomfort of a narrow and shallow communications trench until we caught up with Summers who was at the head of his squad.

"Where's Turlo?" I asked.

"He's out there." Summers pointed in the direction of the airport. "Just follow me. I'm going right out there."

We squatted under a stunted, straggling palm for a few seconds. Then we stood up, glanced in the direction from which the machine gun fire was coming and ran toward the airfield. I waited until he was halfway across the open stretch of ground and then I followed.

He plunged into a shell hole; Turlo's squad was there, along with the platoon guide, Boudrie, and the platoon commander. They were trying to plan our lines, but it was obvious they had no contact to the right and they talked of positions and of digging in but nothing could be done.

Word was passed along for us to move up to the front lines and one by one in the gathering darkness, cursing at holes and wire and roots and each other, we filed out of the crater and climbed the ridge to the airfield terrace.

And we said, although it was our first night of digging in, "By God, if this isn't just like the Marine Corps—waiting until dark to dig in until you can't see a God damn thing."

And the word came down the line "Pass the word back to move to the right; pass the word; pass the word, passtheword passthewordpasspasspass. . . ." They gave us our landmark, too—"You'll see a dead Marine up there—Matthews, you ought to know him: Mac Ferguson—and that'll be our area across the open ridge."

I didn't know any Mac Ferguson. But I did know the little blond MacPherson who lay dead on the ridge where a Jap gunner had cut him down.

And we dug in on the ridge beyond MacPherson, for that was our sector.

6

The full black of the night was upon us when we arrived at our positions and it hung about us oppressively like a shroud for we were nervous and, because we hadn't dug in, a little frightened.

Under the normal formula we could expect a counter-attack; just after sunset and just before dawn were the times when the enemy liked best to strike, they said. We milled about in our defense area, the uniforms of the troops light and ghostly, almost luminous, in the darkness. And the nervousness was expressed in the sharp angry tones of the officers when they addressed each other or their men.

For, it seemed, they sometimes failed to get the word also. And they fretted and cursed when they saw that troops on the right flank under the angry cliffs had withdrawn in the direction of the beach and they held up the stabilization of our own sector until they saw what was planned on the flank.

To the left the anfractuosity which was our line existed as far as we could see along the airport terrace ridge. We could see some of the men digging in on the edge of the airfield itself, but most of them had scooped out foxholes along the side of the terrace so that their heads could protrude above the ridge line, if necessary.

The word came up that the right flank was not pulling back: the apparent withdrawal was only a concerted rush for supplies of chow and ammunition which had just come up. The front had stabilized itself now and we were put into line. My squad's position marked the hinge of our defense as it turned from the edge of the airport and twisted its way down to the beach. Three men—Rice, the only BAR-man left in the squad, Seiden and Laramie—were installed in a foxhole on the flat ground at the top of the terrace where the embankment made an L-turn from an east-west to a north-south direction. This position looked north toward the enemy lines on the left of the cliffs and it was so situated that it could protect not only against an attack down the taxiway but it could guard against Japs who might try to sneak into our lines along the north-south terrace embankment.

The remainder of our squad was put into a large shell hole to the rear and slightly to the right of this position. We not only could protect the rear of this pivotal point but had good firing positions against anything east of the embankment. Five men—Kennedy, Koon, Beeson, West and I, all riflemen—were in this hole and Turlo after placing us here withdrew to a foxhole about five yards beachward on our right. To the right of his hole and approximately the same distance away was a machine gun position, and slowly the rest of the line, which stretched thus across the entire length of the island occupied by us, was built up.

We were now a firm defense, we thought, anchored

from water's edge to water's edge, but we did not really know any of this for we were not informed of the success of the strategy as a whole and all we knew was what we could see, which often was only a distance of twenty feet or so from rim to rim of our shell holes. But we felt we were secure in our own rights and we began to relax somewhat.

Our security measures were not complete, however. A machine gunner, stooping low, ran into our shell hole from the right. In his hand he carried a ball of thin, strong white cord which he unrolled behind him as he ran.

"Grab a hold," he said and someone seized the cord. He spoke briefly to Kennedy and Koon and darted out of our position and up the terrace to the foxhole on the hinge and from there he ran to the left, working his way from shelter to shelter until he disappeared from view.

"What's the idea of this?" I asked.

"It's a sort of alarm cord. If you want to get out of the hole, you jerk on it three times to let the men on either side of you know so you won't get shot. But if you see a Jap you jerk if five times or more—just pull like hell—to let them know what's up."

One of us continued to hold onto the cord while the others talked over the problems of establishing a watch for the night. No one needed to impress us with the importance of an alert guard and the discussion was not of the necessity but of the means. It was agreed that at least two men should be on watch at all times and that the length of each watch should be two hours. That would mean that, for us, two men would watch and three sleep. At the end of two hours the three sleepers would be awakened and they would take over, allowing their two predecessors to sleep. It was not a good system, for a staggering of the watch would have allowed two men to be on guard while three men slept at all times, but we thought then only of maximum protection and not of systems and we were satisfied.

Beeson and Koon took the first watch and I unrolled my poncho. I lay on my left side against the lower portion of the hole, and by twisting and hunching my body I half-buried myself in the still warm sand, then spread the poncho over me. I was asleep almost immediately.

When I awoke I realized it was not the changing of the watch but the cold which had interrupted my sleep. My poncho, which I had pulled over myself as I lay on the slope, had slipped off. I was shivering violently. I pulled the big rubberized garment over me and lay looking at the stars, and the moon which now was shining and I wondered at the ability of a man to sleep when every instinct should tell him to remain awake. I asked Beeson, who sat to my right and whose head and shoulders protruded well above the rim of the pit, if anything had happened and he replied shortly that everything was quiet. Still shivering, I buried my head under the poncho, tucked it tightly about me so that no gleam would show, and lighted a cigarette.

The smoke, which had no way of escaping, almost choked me, but it was warm and I dragged on the cigarette until my fingers were scorched. I then thrust the butt into the sand and, with my head still covered, I again fell asleep.

I felt that I had barely nodded when a hand on my shoulder waked me. It was Beeson.

"Time to take over the watch."

I lay still a moment until my head cleared and he sat above me, watching me silently. I lifted myself to my elbow and he said:

"There're just two ponchos in this hole. Mind if I use yours while you're on watch?" I noticed then for the first time that Kennedy was sleeping uncovered to my left.

"Sure, help yourself."

I threw off the poncho and my body seemed to drain of warmth. I shivered violently as I inched my way to the top of the hole. I scooped a niche in the sand and I sat on my right hip but the sand shifted from beneath me and I had to dig both feet into the side for support to keep my feet from slipping down.

"Keep your head up and your eyes open," Beeson said, "or one of those little bastards will get in here sure as hell."

I needed no urging. The sleep which had fallen easily and lightly over me was gone and I felt refreshed. I held the white cord in my right hand and looked northward along the embankment below the foxhole of the other members of the squad and I searched the ground to the right of the bank, sweeping an area of approximately fifty yards across the highest ground in the open space.

The darkness was pushed back by flares which were thrown up by our mortars and by ships' guns. The naval flares were almost as disconcerting as enemy shellfire until you became accustomed to them. You heard first the sizzling rise of the flares, followed by the sharp report of the gun's discharge and, almost immediately, the burst of the flare shell high above. And the flare casing raised a whining wail like a mammoth piece of shrapnel as it fell empty to the ground. I have heard of men who were killed by the falling cases but I never saw any. These flares were fired so that they burst in front of our lines and the casings, when they fell, normally struck in or near enemy lines.

And the night moved in and out, in and out as the flares burned and died and more were fired into the air and the revolving light beneath the parachute cast a rotating black shadow on the low-hanging clouds. Sometimes the flares helped you to see in front of you, but sometimes you felt, when the wind carried them behind you, that they only silhouetted your head and shoulders for any Jap to see and you wanted to shrink inside your hole but you dared not move.

But nothing stirred in front of you and you were aware that the line was well alerted and you were thankful. For you could see the heads and the shoulders of other men moving in all the foxholes on either side of you as far as you could follow the line and you remembered that the others here were as vitally concerned with maintaining this watch as you were. It was later in the campaign, they used to tell you, when you had to be careful, for men tired out from a day's fighting would fall asleep on watch even when they knew the sleep might cause their death. You remembered then the tale they used to tell about Hopper when he was in the Saipan campaign. Hopper was a good man and they used to say he's sort of old for this sort of thing but he's rugged. He was a good, careful man, they said—the sort you liked to have around you—and on Saipan he not only kept a vigilant watch forward for the Japs but also an eye to the flanks for those heads and shoulders bobbing in adjoining foxholes, for he realized that one man cannot see everything. And when he failed to see a head jutting from a shelter he merely raised his rifle and fired two or three rapid urgent shots into the air, or threw a grenade well out in front, and it did as much to alert the sector as a *banzai* attack would have done. The heads and shoulders would come into view again.

I wondered again about the condition of my rifle but I did not want to make the noise which opening and shutting the bolt would have caused. Not knowing whether it was necessary but not wanting to take any chances I brushed around the bolt and the operating rod handle and groove. It made me feel better and it helped exhaust my two hours of duty.

The minutes passed surprisingly quickly so that I was startled when West whispered that our time was up. He and Kennedy and I slid into the bottom of the crater and awakened Beeson and Koon and they took our places.

My coldness had become not a mere tremor but an ache and I almost dropped my rifle as I placed it, operating rod handle away from the sand, so that it leaned against my gas mask carrier. I burrowed into the sand again, higher in the hole this time, so that Beeson could drape part of the poncho over his legs, but I was still cold, for the sun-warmth of the sand was gone. I smoked another cigarette and my muscles relaxed and I fell asleep on my left side with my face in the sand and my helmet, its strap still buckled, pulled as far as possible over the right side of my head.

I woke with a violent start. Sand poured under the edge of my helmet and over my face. I felt a violent blow on my shoulder and I jumped to my feet.

"*Get* your God damn head down!" Beeson yelled. I ducked and simultaneously heard the pop and whine of a bursting grenade. Two rifles fired near my head and another grenade exploded and the shrapnel whistled overhead.

I trembled violently as though giant unseen hands shook each muscle.

I seized my rifle and climbed, stumbling and crawling, up the side of the hole beside Beeson. I thrust my head above the side and something ripped into the sand by my face so close that the grains stung my right cheek. I ducked involuntarily but raised my head again and sighted along my rifle in the direction from which I thought the grenade bursts had come.

But even as I sighted I knew that if I fired the muzzle blast would deafen Beeson for my position was such that my rifle pointed directly over his shoulder.

I shifted my body so that I had an open field of fire but even then I was uncertain that I should be any good against attackers. I shook so violently that I could barely hold my rifle and my entire body vibrated so that I pressed close to the sand for steadiness.

I looked out to the right and I saw something move near the ground and I jerked violently at the white cord which lay in front of me. Another flare went up and I saw that the movement was that of a small bush ruffled by the brisk breeze. I felt sheepish but I did nothing to quiet the alert I had caused by the jerking of the string. Everyone was awake in the nearby holes, anyhow.

I still could not determine the cause for the outburst of fire and I asked Beeson what he had seen.

"We got a Jap," he said.

"Where?"

"Right out there," and he pointed toward the foot of the embankment in front of us. I had been looking too far out but now, barely 20 feet in front of us, I could see a dark bundle lying on the ground and when a flare came down a helmet glinted.

"Is he dead?"

"Yeh. I think so. But if he's not and makes another move he soon will be. Keep your eyes open out to the right. I think there's another out there."

Sleep was out of the question for any of us now and we lined the front and side of our crater and stared out into the night which turned from yellow to black and back to yellow again. And I remembered every story I had ever heard of the Jap trick of playing dead, so that when I should have been looking to the right I found myself staring at the man lying in front of us and I had to force myself to scan the other ground nearby. But his position never changed and I began to be convinced that he was dead.

Far off to the right I could hear the rest of the line becoming uneasy. A machine gun rattled unsteadily in a short burst followed by a long one and a BAR with its slower shuttling fire joined in. The firing reached a crescendo when the flat cracks of several rifles sounded but it died away quickly only to be renewed again and the line came alive in these outbursts. The heads and the shoulders along the line stayed above ground and twisted and turned automatically as the men studied the terrain before and about them.

We maintained the full watch until the sky in the east became gray and then bright and suddenly the day was with us. The Jap before us was in full view now and it was obvious that he was dead and our minds relaxed and we felt good. Even I, who had nothing to do with his death, somehow felt victorious.

Beeson's silence left him and he laughed.

"I had a hell of a time with that grenade," he said.

"I pulled on it and pulled on it and I just couldn't get the f——g pin out. I finally had to bite the damn thing down with my teeth.

"And all the time I was pulling I was yelling to Koon, 'Get 'im, Zeke; get 'im. Get the bastard!' "

Zeke laughed.

"And I was shaking so hard I didn't know whether I could hit anything if I did fire," he said.

"The pin came out all of a sudden and I threw the grenade at him and it knocked him down when he was running for the hole but he got up and started to run again and we both shot at the same time and he fell again."

"But where did that other grenade come from?"

"I don't know; maybe Seiden threw it."

Seiden, attracted by the talking in our shelter, emerged from his hole atop the embankment and raced down and joined us. He sat back on his heels and grinned.

"To hell with you guys."

"What's the matter?"

"You got my God damn Jap. I was sitting up there on watch with Laramie and I thought I saw something move out below me. I looked hard—I thought it might be a Marine who had gotten out of our lines—and I saw the helmet glint under a flare and I said, 'Oh-oh! That's a Jap.'

"The son of a bitch was in a shell hole and just as I realized what he was doing he jumped out and squatted there in the open in a little shallow trench and looked all around him. I guess he was trying to find our lines.

"I raised my rifle and aimed at him and squee-ee-eezed the trigger—and the damn thing misfired." Excitement gripped him so that as he talked, spit bubbled at the corners of his mouth. "He heard it and looked up and threw a grenade and I ducked. The next thing I knew, you had him."

"Then that wasn't your grenade—that second one?"

"No. I thought both of them came from this hole. The one he threw at me was a dud; it's sticking in the dirt just outside our hole."

Seiden made a show of mock anger, shook his head and repeated: "To hell with you guys."

"I guess Bee and I've got credit for half a Jap apiece, haven't we?" Zeke said. Beeson laughed and agreed.

We chatted a short while and Seiden departed. One by one, worried by the failure of Seiden's rifle to function, we went up the terrace and fired test rounds in the direction of a ridge across the taxiway. We presumed it was occupied by the enemy and we could always hope that one of our bullets might strike someone. My rifle fired but failed to feed after the first round. I put a second round in the chamber manually and fired again; again it failed to feed.

I slid down off the terrace and returned to our shell hole but before I entered it I walked over and looked at the Jap. He looked pitifully small and it was easy to see whose grenade the second one had been. It was his own.

He lay on his back and his arm were flung wide. Both hands were gone and what had been his chest was now a gaping hole with small bits of ribs sticking out of the torn flesh. He was wounded also in both legs and across his left hip. These last wounds evidently were caused by the bullets and the grenade from our hole.

81

Two other Marines walked up and stood over the Jap. One of them put the toe of his boot under the body and turned it over and they explored his pockets. One found a small battle flag and the other, with his combat knife, severed the leather belt to which hung the Jap's bayonet.

We turned and walked to the shell hole, I sat down and field-stripped and cleaned my rifle on my poncho, and the word came up that Turlo had been evacuated for treatment of his wounded shoulder.

7

"Pass the word along to stand by to move out."

We repeated the sentence to the hole on our left and heard it being repeated down the hill toward the beach, fading to sibilants in the distance.

The two Marines with their loot from the dead Jap darted out toward their own shelter and the members of my squad entered ours and began donning their gear. I assembled my rifle hurriedly, thinking this is the way it always happens; you get started on something and you immediately get the word to move out. But I was only dramatizing a fancied plight for my own entertainment because it was the first time such a thing had happened to me.

I rolled my poncho and the brilliant orange front line panels into a tight and compact bundle which I suspended from the rear of my cartridge belt by heavy twine, and I shrugged my way again into the suspenders which held the belt. I ducked low in the hole and removed my helmet and the fatigue cap beneath it, so that I could slip my gas mask carrier over my head and onto the back of my shoulders. I replaced the headgear

83

and reflected that this made only the second time in more than twenty-four hours that it had been off my head. The first time had been last night when I removed the carrier. The helmet had become almost a part of me so that I felt naked and uncomfortable when I removed it.

I replaced the assistant BAR-man's belt on my left side, examined the grenades which I had shoved into the deep sand near my head last night, and put them into the make-shift carrier which I had contrived from the belt. When I had donned the bandoliers which hung crossed over my chest I was ready to move out at a moment's notice and I sat down in the hole, raised the gas mask carrier until the back of my neck fitted against it comfortably, leaned back, and lighted a cigarette.

We talked little but were content to take it easy. None of us had slept much the night before and we rested, relaxed in our minds as well as in our bodies. The Japanese mortars and artillery were beginning to fall again but the shells were not striking close to our lines. Our own artillery, which the veterans explained was pack howitzers, was firing over our heads and the shells fell far forward along the taxiway. I remembered the admonition of Sergeant Summers who had advised me to learn as quickly as possible the difference between the Japanese and our own artillery and I listened closely.

Our guns, several hundred yards to the rear, fired in batteries of four at a time. The discharges came not quite simultaneously so that we heard first the long, drawn out sizzling, then the faint flat chunk of the muzzle discharges followed closely by the smashing

84

roar of the four explosions ahead of us.

But the sizzling continued, for by the time the projectiles from the first battery had fallen a second battery had fired and the shells were passing overhead, one after the other.

The veterans looked up and grinned. They were proud of the 75-millimeter weapons which had proved invaluable in previous campaigns.

"But just you wait," one of them said, "until the one-oh-fives come in and get going. They'll heckle the Jap artillery into a duel and then you'll see something.

"On Saipan they came ashore late the first day. The next day they fired at the Japs until a Jap artillery piece would answer and then—wham! they'd knock the hell out of it. They didn't waste any time about it, either."

Our naval vessels were also firing heavily again, and I had not yet learned to identify their fire. I still ducked involuntarily when they fired because they seemed to be almost in the hole with me. Their projectiles had so much more velocity than the artillery's that there was no sound of the intermediate sizzle; there was just the crack of the discharge and then the roar of the explosion as the projectiles struck their targets.

And I flinched violently, at the discharge of our rockets which were fired from the very beginning of the campaign from ships and planes. Even now the planes were over our heads, diving down on the cliffs one at a time, with the vicious sibilance of their rockets being followed by the grinding snarl of machine guns as they ended their dives with strafing runs.

The rockets from the ships came sometimes in strings of perhaps hundreds and turned the face of the cliffs into a seething, boiling mass of debris and smoke.

85

The plane rockets, usually fired in bursts of six from each fighter, were even more terrifying because they were nearer to us.

Now the whole angry chorus was being sung over and about us. But it was mostly our song and the sound of it was sweet in our ears. We were almost jovial when we spoke, although we spoke seldom.

But even the small talk of our hole died down as the minutes dragged into an hour and we had not moved. What was causing the hold-up? We did not know and our uncertainty made us nervous.

And then came the electrifying cry:

"Stand by for a tank attack!"

Stand by for a tank attack stand by for a tank attack standbystandbytankstankstanks, the words screamed and whispered their way down the hill and we stood up in our holes and milled thoughtlessly, for we were in no position to meet tanks and we knew it.

An officer strode swiftly by and spoke to our platoon noncommissioned officers and the sight of him quieted the troops who nevertheless continued to stand.

"The platoon is going to pull back here," one of the noncommissioned officers said, and he pointed to another terrace about thirty yards to the rear. "We are going to post spotters along this ridge, and the rest of us are going to set up our lines back here."

He glanced about.

"Koon! Matthews! You get up here on the right and watch everything ahead of you and to the right. There'll be somebody else to watch the left. For God's sake keep your eyes open. If you see anything coming give us the word and then run like hell. Do you understand?"

I nodded mutely.

"Get up there now," he repeated, "and keep your eyes open."

I walked slowly up the bank and my legs felt stiff and foreign to my body. I scooped out a hollow on the right side of the incline almost directly above the spot where the dead Jap lay and I sat with my back to him watching the ground which was level for approximately a hundred yards in front of me. Beyond that it gave way to a series of abrupt low hills which were covered with scrub trees of a kind which I could not determine at the distance.

Koon had climbed the bank at the same time I had and he sat in the foxhole which had been occupied the night before by Seiden, Laramie, and Rice. He was about five yards from me. Approximately twenty-five yards to our left I could see two other spotters from our platoon, Sergeant Adams and Corporal Degliequi. They stood together on the ridge line which lay behind me, and the upper half of their bodies stood out plainly.

Corporal Sibisky of the first platoon, looking extremely small and thin in his heavy gear, scrambled up the terrace back of me and crawled into the hole with Koon. They chatted together for a few minutes and then Sibisky turned and, crouching low, ran to the place occupied by the other spotters. I left my hole on the side of the embankment and raced over to join Koon.

As I dropped into the foxhole which was shallow and wide I felt water on the side of my face. Another drop struck me and then it began to rain slowly and steadily. A chill wind blew across the open ground and the rain beat in our faces and I buttoned my combat jacket around my neck. I lowered my face against the rain and then, realizing I could not maintain a watch with my eyes to the ground, I lifted my head and the water trickled to the tip of my nose where it clung coldly. I blew upward and spattered it, but another drop formed in its place and then fell aggravatingly. I tried to brush it away with my hands but they were covered with sand which transferred to my face, making me more uncomfortable than ever. And I noticed that where my hands had touched my rifle the sand and dust from my hands had been transformed into a thin mud which the rain was dissolving and spreading along the hand guard and operating rod. I was angry and nervous, for it looked as if I might need the weapon soon, and I cursed but there was nothing I could do about it. I wiped each hand under the opposite armpit and dabbed ineffectually at my rifle with the dry underside of my right forearm.

And as I sat I turned cold. I was sitting in an almost squatting position with my heels pressed tight against my buttocks and the rain dampened and then drenched my dungarees along my thighs and the water seeped through and trickled down my upturned legs to my crotch. I shivered and stretched my legs in front of me and the wet trousers which had not heretofore touched below my knees settled and clung to them. My faint shivers turned to violent tremors like those which I had experienced during the killing of the Jap soldier at night and I clenched my fingers about the stock of my rifle to keep the trembling from showing.

But I noticed then that Koon was trembling also and that his lips had turned a blue-gray. I unbuttoned my combat jacket and brought out a cigarette and lighted it. He took one and I held out my cigarette to give him a light and we both trembled so violently that we missed contact. I laughed.

"This would be funny as hell," I said, "if it weren't so damned unfunny."

He smiled.

"You ain't kiddin'." He paused. "How'd you like a good hot cup of joe?"

"How'd *you* like a good hot tom 'n' jerry?" I replied.

"And how'd you like a rifle butt in the mouth?"

We laughed and felt better, for the laughter had relaxed our nerves. But we still shivered and now we knew we shook from the cold.

"Last night," I said, "I couldn't make up my mind whether I was shaking from the cold of the weather or from the heat of the action."

He said he'd been the same and we chatted briefly but our talk died, for over our heads came the sizzling of our battery fire and the hills before us shook and spewed smoke and dirt high in the air. The sizzling continued, a full scale barrage in which the ships, now moved close to the shore under the cliffs, joined. And our mortars, also firing in batteries, became active, cleaving the air behind us with their s-s-s-schunk-s-s-s-schunk . . . chunk-chunk-s-s-s and the ground vibrated as the barrage moved in from the hills toward us and then moved back again so that the shells fell out of sight beyond the rise in the ground.

And we nudged each other and pointed gleefully as a column of black smoke built up solidly beyond the hills, for in our mind's eye we could see a tank burning and we said to ourselves that's one of the bastards out of the way. But in truth we saw no tanks and, for that matter, no Japs, although Koon started suddenly and

89

swore he had seen a soldier tumble down inside a shell hole about two hundred yards from us. He even professed to see footprints down the side of the hole. It was on an incline so that we could see into it and I imagined I could see them too.

But we were silenced suddenly as the barrage came back across the hills and dug at the open space before us, some of the shells striking within fifty yards of us and we burrowed as deep as possible into the foxhole, lifting our heads to continue our watch only when the sizzling of the falling shells stopped and the whine of the shrapnel died away.

The sand in front of our hole danced and spat with our own shrapnel and the unintentional barrage was as dangerous to us atop the crest as if it had been thrown down by the Japanese. But it moved away again and Koon and I sat up and looked about.

The spotters to our left were gone. The hill was bare except for us.

"Wait here and I'll see what the scoop is," Koon said. He sprinted out of the hole and down the embankment and I turned again to watch the front. He reappeared in a short while.

"Come on down," he shouted and returned to the platoon's positions. I followed him.

"Adams has been hit," he said. "In the face. Pretty bad, I think."

The sergeant, his helmet off, lay on his left side on the rear embankment. About him clustered four or five friends, the platoon leader, and Scala the corpsman. Adams' face was as gray as the sand on which he lay and his eyelids fluttered feebly. A great flow of blood seeped from his cheek and neck and pooled into the ground under his chin. The corpsman was preparing an injection of blood plasma and another man had been sent for litter bearers when I turned toward my squad.

The rain had stopped but the clouds still hung low and heavy and the squad lay huddled in twos and threes just below the crest of the bank. The groups were spread about ten yards apart and most of them had dug shallow pits against the slope. About thirty yards to the left the terrace made an L-turn to the rear, and below us, under the protection of this declivity, was a tank. Members of the crew in their helmets stood by or walked slowly about the vehicle, eyeing and fingering holes in the armor plating along the sides and rear. The tank was out of commission and had been brought to this position for repairs.

I scooped a hole out of the side of the bank and lay in it, my face to the rear. I could see others from our platoon clustered on top of the embankments behind our last night's position.

As I watched, our artillery and mortar barrage against the Jap lines across the taxiway dwindled and died away. Suddenly the air sizzled again and I thought we're still at it, for it was obvious that this was battery fire, but as I watched to our rear the ground spouted up in a line from the airport down to a point near where our platoon had advanced inland from the beach. This time it was Japanese fire; their guns, too, were being used in batteries.

And the thought struck me that the enemy had spotted this tank below us and was trying to destroy it and I unbuckled my entrenching tool which was fastened to my cartridge belt and widened and deepened my hole so that nothing short of a direct hit in the hole or on top of the tank would endanger me. But suddenly I knew I had figured wrong for the next salvo, and the next, hit in approximately the same location and it became obvious that the enemy, stung by our barrage, was seeking out not this tank but our artillery. I sat up in my hole and looked about.

Apparently most of the men thought as I did that we were in no immediate danger. But the man on my right continued to dig, stopping when the air above us was quiet but renewing his work when the sizzling occurred until finally, under a heavy outburst, he dropped his entrenching tool and, bending down, frantically scooped at the ground with his hands, flinging the sand, dog-fashion, between his legs. I pitied him because he obviously needed to learn about artillery fire even more than I did.

But the mortars did find us and they probed inquisitive fingers about for the tank until our platoon leaders gave the word for us to scatter away from the area surrounding the vehicle. We moved toward an embankment to our right and lay flat against the side of this hill.

I was there when Matchunis walked over and sat beside me. He was troubled.

"I guess you know that Lieutenant H—— has been killed?"

I had not heard this and I was sorry, for the lieutenant was known throughout our company as a fine officer. A huge, blond man with an emotionless face, he had been unpopular when he first joined the company, for he was, the men complained, too GI—a stickler for spit and polish. But after the Saipan-Tinian operations he was as admired as much as he previously was disliked; there he proved himself to be a fair and fearless man.

"Captain Harshbarger got it, too," Matchunis continued. "Not too badly, I think, but he had to turn in.

"Matty," he continued, "I think I've got a charmed life."

"How's that?"

"Yesterday I was running with another feller for a shell hole. We both dived for the hole just as a shell burst near us. I made it, but he didn't. He had an arm blown off. I wasn't scratched.

"And then I was standing between two other guys when a mortar shell hit close to us. Both of them got it pretty bad but again I wasn't scratched. That was twice in one day."

"Our c.p. was hit earlier today and the top got it," (that also was news to me) "and then they set up another temporary c.p. near some tanks and the Japs started hitting at those and that's when Lieutenant H—— and Captain Harshbarger got it. I was standing right next to H—— when he was hit and I didn't get touched. But I'm afraid my luck is going to play out on me."

"How about the top; was he hurt badly?"

"Yeh. I hear he may lose an arm and a leg."

Matchunis rose to his feet and started away.

"Take it easy," I said.

Take it easy. It was the universal *vale* of this operation: a farewell clothed in concern but decorated with an air of calm carelessness. It was affected by everyone. What it meant, of course—and we all knew it—was just the opposite of what it said. For we didn't mean take it easy. We meant, instead, keep your tail down and your eyes open and run like hell. Take it easy? Oh, no!

8

We moved cautiously, for we were in territory new to us and we were afraid of mines. A demolitions outfit had gone through ahead of us at some previous time and had marked the mine fields but the mines still were there and in the growing dusk of the late afternoon it was difficult to see the tatters of cloth on the sticks marking the explosives.

And because we were uncertain of our territory we not only walked cautiously but we talked in the same manner. We were firm believers in passing the word and now the information and the warnings passed down the line slowly, working their way stumblingly from man to man.

"Heads down—open space up forward," it ran and the soft hisses of the s's slithered up to you and resolved themselves into words, then faded meaninglessly as they passed by you and to the men in the rear.

"Stay in the trenches—mines ahead," and the muscles tightened in our legs and our arms and our stomachs.

Our rules of quiet were broken only in emergencies and the entire line screamed in anxious, wrathful indignation when we saw three men unconcernedly walking across the fields which we had so carefully skirted. Our words were an invisible wall in front of them with their unconcern turning to bounding fright when they realized the meaning of the cloth-covered sticks past which they had been walking.

Like our words our steps ranged from the silent and cautious to the pounding and impetuous and we stormed in twos and threes and fours across the open spaces, taking advantage of each shell hole. It was in one of those, occupied temporarily by members of my platoon, that I came across the second Japanese I had seen on the island. Like the first he was dead, and in the same manner. His arms were mutilated and his hands missing but the cavity in his body from the blast of his grenade was lower—across his belly so that portions of his intestines hung over his legs.

"Watch the mine," someone said and I saw almost at the Jap's feet a wooden, box-like affair bound with cloth tape and with a detonator protruding from a hole in the wood. It was not until later that I learned this was no mine but an aerial bomb with an exposed detonator buried in the hole which the enemy believed large enough to attract a sizable unit of Americans. I stepped across the body of the dead soldier and sprinted for the next crater.

I paused there for breath and asked, "What's the scoop?" but the only thing anyone could tell me was that our outfit was moving down to the far right and we were going into the line at that position. Night was not far off and speed was essential so that we could find the lines and dig in before darkness enveloped us.

The column in which we traveled turned abruptly to

the left and began slowly to curl its way from the beach onto the high ground again and even as I darted across a slight knoll into a communications trench I heard the rattle of a machine gun in front of me and I hurled my body against the wall of the trench.

Spurred from the rear, the remainder of the company continued to overrun the communications trench and we shouted back for the others to hold up, but on they came and we cursed and writhed and waved our arms to stop them for fear that the overcrowded shelter would draw fire from the enemy mortars. But more dove in with us and the only thing we could do was to dash for holes ahead, which we did in small, angry groups.

The sharp, light crack of enemy rifles joined in the fire against us, punctuated occasionally by the shrill whine of hand grenades and knee mortars. We flattened ourselves against the ground.

"God damn it," someone to my left growled. "They told us we were going into the front lines. Hell, we *are* the front lines."

It was true. We had been staging a push without knowing it. But we knew it now and we knew that enemy pillboxes lay in front of us.

And we heard shouts ahead of us and rose to our knees to watch. Sergeant Summers and Corporal Degliequi from the second squad were forward of us and had joined battle against one of the emplacements. Behind them and, we thought, engaged in the same action, other members of the squad could be seen.

We heard the steady burst of our semi-automatic rifles followed by the sudden dull discharge of a rifle grenade. We ducked as the fragments flew back over our heads.

As we flinched the ground rose and hit us and the sides of our shell hole fell in about us, pouring sand across our helmets, and the air was heavy with sound.

We looked up to see a black column of smoke and we caught the sight of fragments of some solid material flying even higher than the smoke cloud.

"Demolitions," the man on my left said aloud but he was not talking to me or to anyone other than himself.

"Jesus!" another said. "They really poured it into them then. I wonder what size charge they used? I'll bet there's nothing left of the pillbox."

But there was. When we looked again we saw smoke still issuing into the air and we saw the position of the emplacement clearly for the first time. The squad moved farther up the hill and then split, three men turning to the right and the remainder going directly to the front. The three moved slowly and cautiously toward the pillbox, which appeared to be only a slight rise in the ground. They almost circled it before they stopped and pressed close against its side. The man in front leaned his rifle against the wall and we could see that he was disengaging the pin in the safety lever of a grenade. He lurched forward, threw hard to his left with an underhand motion and the three men scrambled to the near side of the rise and pressed against the ground. We heard an explosion and dust flew from the left of the mound.

The men rose and another one of the three, whom I recognized as Corporal Martel, repeated the performance. Again they raced to safety and this time the explosion was followed by the issuance of thick white smoke from what evidently was the embrasure.

"Phosphorus," said the man at my left.

The remainder of the squad was near the crest of the ridge and the members of it suddenly flattened themselves. Now the singing of enemy grenade fragments was clear but distant to us and we saw their origin. Another Japanese pillbox, also distinguished by little more than a slight rise in the ground, lay at the crest. As we watched, amazed, a Jap jumped high in the air from the rear of the shelter and we saw the arc of his arm as he threw. He was gone from sight before the squad's rifles cracked. And we could hear the angry cries.

"Grenade! Grenade!"

"Get 'im! Get 'im! Get the son of a bitch!"

"Watch him if he tries that again."

"Duke! Get down! That was a Jap grenade."

And the voice of Duke, who had been one of the three attacking the previous emplacement:

"God damn it! Why don't you tell somebody what's going on?"

But he continued to stand, his rifle held as if he were expecting a covey of quail to rise in front of him. The head and arm of the Jap appeared again and four rifles were fired. The men of the squad, directly in front of the pillbox now, continued to stand, as cool as if they, too, were hunting small game, until the grenade struck in front of them and rolled toward them. They dropped to the ground as the missile exploded and then, unharmed, they rose to their knees. The force of a grenade's explosion against the ground is such that most of the fragments are thrown outward and upward; thus a man flattened against the ground a few yards away has at least a fair chance of escaping injury.

A Marine in the center of the line twisted at the ring of his grenade. He threw with a quick overhand snap of the wrist, like a baseball catcher. The grenade disappeared just over the back of the pillbox. Almost immediately the Jap's head and arm appeared again and the grenade flew back into the open and the squad ducked hurriedly, knowing it would explode almost immediately. It did, sounding heavier and more violent than the Jap's.

And the angry cries rose on the tail of the whining of the fragments as the Marines jumped to their feet again.

"Let's get that bastard this time!"

"Watch him!"

"Shoot the son of a bitch!"

Four of the attackers stood side by side in front of the pillbox and others moved to the right and to the left about it. There was no apparent haste nor, except in words, agitation. The attack went forward as it might have in maneuvers except that in practice, exposure such as this ahead of me would have brought instant condemnation from any observing officer.

The faint burst and the shrill crying fragments of another enemy grenade came, and then another, and with them the call:

"Corpsman! Corpsman!"

Someone was hit. I could not see who it was and the voices died as rifle fire exploded again.

It was obvious then that several Japs occupied the pillbox and that the emplacement itself was only one of a series of such defenses which were mutually supporting. This one was protected from the far side of the ridge so that the present small scale flanking attack was useless. The men to the right and left came slowly down from the ridge and the squad as a whole pulled back to the main body of our troops.

Later we found out that Sergeant Summers, in an effort to overrun the pillbox before darkness, had asked for additional troops but the word had never reached those in the rear. Similarly, the destruction of the first strong point had been accomplished almost solely by Summers and Corporal Degliequi simply because the remainder of the platoon had not realized what was occurring. Summers had stumbled on the enemy who, from the shelter of a communications trench, were watching us move up. He was joined by Degliequi who forced the enemy into the pillbox through use of a rifle grenade. There one of them, wounded by Summers, blew himself up. That was the "demolition" charge which had shaken us. But the break in our down-the-line communications system which we had tried so vigorously to maintain had been costly in time and, perhaps, in men.

The light had begun to fail and darkness would fall soon. The platoon leaders mustered their troops to prepare to dig in for the night and they plotted a line which would run along the side of the hill barely fifty yards below the unconquered enemy defense outpost.

The frustration of the assault served to add to our confusion. Perhaps, basically, the confusion came from ignorance of our position. We had moved considerably that day but just why we were where we were few below the rank of platoon leader had any inkling. Whether or not the leaders planned consciously to keep the peons (as we called ourselves) concerned only with the immediacies, that, in the end, was the way it worked. They said "Move out to the right'' and we moved out to the right, knowing that and nothing else; they said ''Dig in here'' and in we dug, conscious of what was ahead of us only when the thing ahead fired at us. Perhaps somewhere on somebody's map the actions of our company made a pretty pattern against the whole picture, but what the readers of those maps probably didn't know was that it was a pretty pattern of desperate little confusions.

The nervousness we felt at being caught midway between the offensive and the defensive descended upon us, too, and we milled in the growing dusk while we were assigned points at which to dig.

''You, S——, take your squad and build up from this point across this little knoll and make contact with the third platoon on your right.''

''God *damn* it, can't you make up your mind? I dug in once and then was told to move over there. Now you want me to move again.'' And, to members of his squad he said: ''You may as well stop digging—but damn it don't leave this place. I'm going to find out something definite for once.''

But this latest order was confirmed by an officer and the squad leader, petulant in his anger, ordered his men to their new positions.

And so our lines built up unsteadily, for it was not just the unpleasantness of additional work but a matter of personal safety which intervened and in this matter the troops felt they could make themselves heard. And they did.

One platoon leader pointed to a wooden knoll just forward of the captured Japanese pillbox. It was dense with the stunted palms which marked the greatest part of the vegetation of the island.

102

"K——, send two of your men to that knoll so they can watch the draw up here to the left. Build the rest of your squad up from there over to here. Put two men to a hole."

And K—— turned to two veterans. It was obvious that he thought the position dangerous.

"How about it," he asked, "will you two set up out there?"

"Hell, no, I won't," B—— replied promptly. "I'm not gonna ask to be bumped off. You know damned well—and I know you know it—that there's no way in God's world to dig in up there. They'd knock us off like clay pigeons. No. I'm not going out there."

The squad leader turned back to the platoon leader.

"How about just to the left of the knoll," he asked, "with another hole to the right? Then you'd have protection in every direction without unnecessary exposure."

"Sure, that's all right. But for God's sake, let's get something done. We'll be standing around here all night long with our pants down."

And the concern with personal safety showed elsewhere.

"For Christ's sake, we're in a hell of a spot here. We ought to have more than two men to a hole. How about seeing if he won't change it to put three men together so that two can be on watch all the time?"

"No, we can't do that. Our lines are too thin as they are. Look how far apart these holes are."

"Well, look at all the troops they have in reserve back there. Why can't they move some of those men up here to fill it out?"

And so it went and finally they did move some of the

men out of reserve and into the front line, but they still insisted that two men to a foxhole would be sufficient.

They cautioned us tonight to watch toward the rear as well as to the front, for our advance had been swift and makeshift during the afternoon and it was not unlikely that we might have by-passed some enemy positions.

Zeke Koon and I again occupied the same foxhole. To our left and slightly to the rear were West and Laramie and farther along but forward was the hole occupied by Beeson and Kennedy. Kennedy had become, in Turlo's absence, our squad leader.

To our right in a shell hole were two men from another outfit, brought up from reserve to fill in the line; beyond them were Seiden and Rice. About a hundred yards past them the line turned sharply downhill to the right so that it faced the cliff. Already machine guns were firing in that sector.

Koon and I were in a small crater and we dug furiously, trying to enlarge the area to two body widths by about six feet long. We piled the dirt which we excavated along the front and sides but we dug only until the hole was deep enough to allow us, while seated, to see over the parapet. We unrolled my poncho and spread it over us and, in turn, each smoked a cigarette while the other watched. Then we knelt in the hole and studied the surrounding terrain intently. We fixed firmly in mind the location of nearby foxholes and of the line which swerved to the right behind us. I was nervous about a communications trench which came up the hill to within five yards of the rear of the hole for I could not see the bottom of it and I realized that a Jap, by using this trench, could creep to within a few feet of our hole without being seen. From there he could drop grenades on us all night long.

Koon pointed down the trench to a spot about 30 yards to the rear.

"I believe that a Jap would have to expose himself at that point if he was crawling along. We'll just have to keep our eyes on it."

It was small consolation.

Our pack howitzers were busy again as we began the night's watch. The sizzling in the air overhead became almost monotonous and the explosions of the falling shells raced up and down the crest of the cliffs to our right with flaming energy.

We removed our bandoliers and cartridge belts and gas masks and piled them inside the parapet so they would not be silhouetted against the sky. We took our hand grenades from their carriers and, remembering Beeson's trouble of last night, we closed the cotter pins through the safety levers, allowing them to be removed easily if needed.

Koon took the first relief. Each of us was to stand an hour. My wrist watch had become so clogged with sand that it had stopped running and it would be necessary for both of us to use Koon's watch. And at the end of each hour we were to wake the occupants of the hole on our immediate right, neither of them having a watch.

I spread the poncho completely over me, tucking one end of it under my feet and the other about my helmet, which I continued to wear. The poncho was so wide that Koon, sitting up near my feet, was able to cover his legs with it, fighting off some of the chill of the night. Sleep came almost immediately and when the touch of his hand on my leg woke me I felt that I had barely closed my eyes. I sat up and Koon, after admonishing me to be on the alert to the rear, pulled the poncho over his head and stretched out beside me.

The contrast between the warmth of the poncho and the chill of the air threw me into a torturous shivering and I drew an end of the rain cover up as far as my waist. But the tremors continued. I pressed my hands between my legs but my inactivity now only increased my shivering. I pulled my rifle in from the edge of the foxhole and brushed unseeingly at it. I felt that I was doing little to improve the condition of its mechanism but the action of my arms and the concentration of my thoughts on it made me feel better. I was unable even to look at it, for the sight of the communications trench held me in an almost hypnotic state. I could see nothing and finally I turned to stare at the front.

The night was as cloudy as the day had been and the light of the flares swinging beneath their parachutes again painted eerie shadows in the sky above and the clouds seemed to lower at me and then retreat into a void as the light diminished.

I swung my gaze back toward the rear, and my mouth went dry and I could feel the pulse of my temples against my cap. A man, crouched low, was moving rapidly and easily toward my hole.

"Halt!" I shouted. "Who's there?"

There was no answer.

"Halt!" I repeated. "Who's there?"

"Aw, go—— yourself," came the answer and I recognized the voice of L——, a man who had been with me since boot camp. My nervousness resolved itself in anger.

" 'F—— yourself,' hell. God damn it, you'd better

give the password. Somebody's going to put a bullet through you sure as hell. It's a wonder I didn't fire after challenging you once."

Koon, now awake, joined in the angry outburst and the man looked over at us and by the light of a flare we could see him grinning.

"What is the password?" he asked. "Hell, I don't know. Nobody ever told me what it is."

We were astounded, but we told him what it was and he moved off. I was still angry and frightened for I realized how close I had been to shooting him. Such things, I had been told, had happened in previous campaigns and I didn't want it to happen to me. I realized too that the man might have been a Jap; he had been within twenty yards of the rear of our hole before I had seen him. I glued my eyes to the rear.

The hour passed swiftly as did my next hour of sleep, so that when I took over the watch the second time my mind still was drunkenly tired, and as I watched I had to fight to keep my eyes open. My position in the soft sand, I thought, might be too comfortable and I threw off the poncho in the hopes that the cold might wake me. The action did, but the absence of the cover helped not at all so that as soon as I settled down, the drowsiness possessed me again. I rose to my feet and then knelt and lowered my body so that I sat on my heels. The discomfort did what the chill had failed to do, and I remained that way until I felt that the muscles of my thighs would be torn loose. I then knelt first on the left knee and then on the right, and during that time I swept the terrain about me for signs of the enemy.

Sporadic firing continued to the right below me and somewhere off to the left I could hear the nacker-

nackernackernackernack . . . nackernackernacker-nack of the burst of a machine gun, but in my platoon's sector it was quiet. I had seen no sign of life outside the adjoining foxholes.

I woke Koon for his second watch and I whispered to the hole on the right that it was time for them to change also. I received no answer but I was afraid to lift my voice and I scooped up a handful of sand and showered it over the men inside. A startled head jerked upright in the hole; I waved, and a hand responded.

I fell asleep with a rapidity which amounted almost to collapse. I think that then in my exhaustion there was no line of demarcation between waking and sleeping because I started violently and guiltily when I heard the voice of Koon bellow:

"How in hell do you expect to see anything with your damned head below the surface of the ground?"

I sat bolt upright and then I realized he had not been talking to me.

"God!" I said. "You scared hell out of me. I thought I had fallen asleep on watch."

"No, I've been on watch only about twenty minutes—you've got lots more time to sleep. But look over there." He pointed to the shell hole on the right. No head was visible above the rim of the crater.

We rose to our knees and peered into the hole. One of the men was asleep and the other sat at his side, well in the bottom of the crater.

"You know," Koon stage-whispered, "you're in this thing, too. Now, God damn it, how about getting up and watching with us?"

There was no answer, but the helmeted figure crawled up the incline of the hole and lay down, peer-ing toward the front.

108

I was still nervous at the way I had been waked and when I lay down, I pulled the poncho over my head and lighted a cigarette. I snuffed it out in the sand after a few puffs, however, and fell asleep again.

The next time I was waked my reaction was the opposite and I came to my senses slowly although there was urgency in Koon's voice and he was speaking to me.

"Get up, Matt—wake up, wake up! There are Japs in front of us!"

My brain snapped and I was wide awake. I sat up and reached to my left for my rifle.

"Where?"

"I haven't seen any yet, but . . ."

To the left a light explosion sounded and the fragments of a grenade whistled overhead. That, I told myself, was Japanese.

". . . But Kennedy and Bee are having a hell of a time. Look!"

In the yellow light of a flare I could see the two men, standing out of their foxhole, leaning against a knoll. Kennedy lurched forward, threw around the side of the knoll to his left and ducked back to cover. The shrapnel whistled sharply and Beeson threw his rifle to his shoulder and fired twice, rapidly.

A voice farther away to the left shouted:

"Fire! Fire!"

A machine gun near us nackered fretfully and then roared into a long burst and rifles opened up along the line above the position of Kennedy and Beeson. The two continued to stand in the open. They fired heatedly for a moment or two and then Kennedy threw another grenade and they dodged behind the knoll. We could see the flash of fire which preceded the heavy burst before we ducked and when we resumed our positions another and lighter explosion came from our right. We looked in that direction but again we could see no sign of life in front of us.

A voice from the right cried:

"Corpsman! Corpsman! Pass the word down for a corpsman!"

We repeated the call to the left and we heard it wind its way over the hill to the left and lose itself as the firing burst forth again desperately.

But we soon saw the shadowy figure of a man running on top of the knoll and as we watched, the figure lost itself in a hole and the word came down before we saw the figure again:

"Stand by for a corpsman moving down from the left."

The corpsman darted from foxhole to shell hole, pausing occasionally to rest briefly. He stopped in the position to our left but he by-passed us and continued on to the right, his body almost parallel to the ground, his dressings case swinging heavily from his side as he ran.

He stopped on the way back to his own hole.

"It was Rice," he said. "Hit in the shoulder. I don't think it's too bad—just a little piece of shrapnel in the shoulder. I fixed it up and I think it'll be all right until he can go back in the morning.

"I'm pooped," he continued. "I had to run about two hundred yards to get down here." He stretched his feet out before him and we chatted briefly until another burst of firing diverted our attention from each other again. The firing died and the corpsman sprinted off to the left.

The dawn came and we relaxed again, but Koon and

I felt baffled, for in spite of the firing which had raged for more than an hour we had not seen a single Japanese. The hill now looked lifeless in front of us and Rice arose from his shelter two holes away on the right and walked in front of us toward the command post. He carried his BAR on his shoulder.

"They're making me go back to the beach for treatment," he said. "I feel like hell leaving the platoon when we're in this spot, but they're making me go back."

We told him he was foolish to feel that way: he'd be back with us only too soon.

He continued on his way, bulky under his gear, and seven out of our thirteen-man squad were left.

9

The new men moved up in straggling groups, their faces gray and strained in the early morning light, and the word passed along our platoon line, "we're in reserve today," and the tightness slipped from our minds. A mortar barrage which flickered and blazed just over the crest of the ridge in front of us and behind yesterday's stubborn pillbox had died away and with it the strain of the night's watch slackened.

The men were coming from the reserve line of the night before and with them they brought not only news but food. They piled into the foxholes with us until the time came for them to move out, and the group on the right ate from and then passed to us, a large can of snapbeans. I used the point of my combat knife as a spoon and I ate hungrily, for, other than a small portion of a chocolate bar, it was the first food I had had in more than two days. As I swallowed, I realized for the first time how hungry I had been. Koon took but little, explaining that he did not like snaps, but, even cold, they tasted to me as delicious as anything I had ever put in my mouth.

"What do we do now?" I asked Koon.

"We just stay here until the rest of the men move out. When they get out about thirty yards or so we follow them. . . . Oh, we're going to be in on the push, too. But it'll be good not to be at the front of things for a change."

Seiden joined us.

"Get any Japs last night?"

"No. We didn't even see any."

"I got one. . . . I know I did. He was just outside the pillbox up there. I saw the son of a bitch squatting there and I shot at him and I saw him slump over. But he's not there this morning. They must have pulled him off the crest—you know they bury their dead when they get a chance, to keep their casualties from being known."

"Stand by to move out." The word was shouted now.

"We'd better get into our gear," Koon said. "It won't be long before we have to move out, too."

We donned our equipment slowly and laboriously and sat down again, feeling once more the familiar constriction and immobility caused by the extra weight.

"We're moving out—on your feet down there, we're moving out."

We watched curiously as the newcomers arose and looked about indecisively. One by one they stepped out of their holes and stood there, waiting until their comrades joined them, and they fingered their helmets or tested the action of their rifles for a few seconds. It was a fascinating spectacle to me, for it shattered every conception I had had of an attack's being a dashing, furious charge.

The line formed with almost slow-motion clarity and the troops, for the first time facing toward the ridge, walked slowly forward, some crouching as they moved, others standing upright. There was not a sound from the pillbox atop the ridge or from any other point ahead and the men moved with the regularity found on maneuvers.

"Don't bunch up! Keep contact! The guide is right!"

The line opened and closed and opened in accordionlike fashion but on the whole it was cohesive and wellformed and broke up into groups only when it was halted by the leaders who held their right hands into the air, palm forward. Men in the line took up the signal and then they lay flat on the ground or moved quickly to nearby shell holes where they kneeled, almost immobile, looking to the front. The leaders waved their hands forward again and the line formed slowly and worked its way toward the crest.

"We're moving out now," the word passed from mouth to mouth down the line of our foxholes and we stood up and waited until someone made the first move forward. Then we, too, walked slowly up the hill and I searched the terrace ahead but saw nothing except the figures of the men in the first wave. That line halted and ours, too, was ordered to hold it up and I trotted a few steps forward and walked down the side of a shell hole.

On the side of the crater near me was a slab of uncooked meat, almost fleshless, around the ribs of a small pig. The ribs themselves showed plainly and the flies clustered on the flesh and I said to myself those flies soon will be trying to light on our food as we eat and a good run of dysentery will start. I remembered tales which I had heard of the filth in which the

Japanese troops lived—how they scattered uneaten food and old containers about their bivouac areas and voided on the open ground where they lived. I felt a surge of disgust, then scooped up a handful of dirt and threw it over the refuse. And I stopped.

My action had uncovered a scrap of cloth protruding from beneath the flesh. It was a portion of the body of a Jap soldier. My stomach churned and I moved to the right, away from the position. I remembered then the mighty explosion which came during the attack on the first pillbox yesterday and I supposed this must be a part of one of the victims. This Japanese, trapped, had chosen to blow himself to bits rather than be taken by our troops.

It was, it seemed to me, a fantastic as well as horrible way to die. To some it seemed to prove the utter fearlessness of the enemy soldier—he was, some of us said, never afraid to die. But now I thought that it showed not fearlessness but a fear which transcended the natural loathing of death. The enemy could have proved himself heroic to me by another kind of willingness to die. That willingness, however, must be accompanied by the relentless desire on the part of the soldier to sell his body as dearly as possible. Of course this man and his comrades had been trapped. Death undoubtedly was certain for them. But the blast which had torn this man to bits had not injured one of the attacking force. Certainly fearlessness, although it would have resulted in death, could have sold itself for a higher price.

I remembered, too, the soldier who had held the grenade against his chest that first night in front of our shell hole. He was wounded before he committed suicide; that is certain. But was he heroic in his willingness to die? He knew where our hole was: the blasts from Koon's and Beeson's rifles showed him that. Wouldn't a fearless man have thrown that grenade into our hole instead of pressing it to his chest? What could be the fear which motivated such a ghastly action?

My thoughts were interrupted as we moved forward again and I was glad to be out of the hole. The first wave disappeared over the crest ahead of us and we were ordered again to halt our advance. I ran into another shell hole and sat along its side. I could see Koon to my right, not far from the hole I had just left, and he nodded to me.

But our delay this time was longer and I shifted to a half-lying position so that I could watch my leader for signals. Behind my back I heard a rumbling and I looked down the hill and saw a tank approaching. Its turret was open and the head of a member of the crew protruded from it. In front was a group of foot soldiers and I could see that they were examining the ground intently as they walked. The hands of the crewman directed them along the most desirable routes to be taken and they crisscrossed the terrain with their minute study.

The procession moved slowly toward me from the left rear, turned when it came on line with my shelter and beetled directly up the face of the hill. It stopped about ten yards in front of me, the roaring died to a rumble as the motors idled and one of the foot troops conferred with the crewman. He moved off again to the right.

Two other tanks came into view on the hill below me and they moved until they had closed the distance between themselves and the first vehicle to a few feet and they too stopped. One was on a line and to the left of my hole; the other slightly to the rear.

The air sighed and the earth erupted with a roar to my right and sand showered about me as I scrambled into the bottom of the pit. I hugged the ground and it heaved again and I held my breath as the shrapnel screamed discordantly. But as I let out my breath I cursed for I could see the antenna of the tank ahead of me and it was not moving. Are they going to sit there, again, I asked myself, are they going to sit there and take it? And make us take it with them? Why must they continually pull up right in the middle of troops and sit? I thought irrationally. Another shell struck and another and another and the last was closer than the first so that it punctuated the unfinished wail of the earlier fragments.

I was angry and I was excited but my mind was clear and I knew—a fact which I would have known even with less clarity of mind—that my position was dangerous and I peered over the edge of the hole to try to find my platoon sergeant. I could see no moving figure in that direction and I ducked back into the hole. Shells fell again and after the detonation I looked to my right and Koon saw me and motioned me to move down the hill in the direction of last night's lines. Even as I watched, Seiden, to Koon's right, arose from the ground and raced crouching toward the rear and disappeared into another shell hole.

The whisper came again and I ducked quickly and pressed my face into the earth and the blast poured sand about me and into the neck of my jacket. I jumped to my feet and dashed into the open in the direction of the hole where I had seen Koon. He was not there but as I jumped into the cover I saw him with Seiden farther below. I arose and darted in that direction and even as I moved I realized that the first tank had been hit. I saw the tread on the right side was dangling loosely. It had been torn apart.

I joined Koon and Seiden in the crater and we sat together near the bottom and pressed our bodies against the sides. I looked about and saw the top of a knoll about twenty feet away and I lowered my body until I lay almost flat and no longer could see the little crest. I had learned that splinters from a shell striking any ground which I could see could hit me but if I could see no surrounding high ground it was unlikely that I should be struck by anything other than a direct hit on my shelter. In the type of warfare we were fighting there was no protection against direct hits.

The barrage continued to play about the damaged tank and then moved, first by a long leap and then by adjusting steps, toward the second. Again our shelter was close to the line of fire and one by one we threaded our way down hill until we were in the positions which we had occupied last night. Even as we settled down, the earth rolled and a black cloud of the volcanic sand belched into the sky above us. We clung to the ground as another shell struck nearby.

"By God, they aren't shooting at those tanks, now. The bastards have spotted us. They're after us, too." Although that seemed indisputable then, it was an illogical assumption.

Koon peered over the edge of the shell hole, seized his rifle and sprinted into the open. I ran up the edge after him, but as I got to the top I heard that deadly sibilant. I let my body crumple, a shell exploded, and I rolled back into the crater. Seiden hurried to my side, his face wrinkled with concern.

"Are you hit?" he asked.

I shook my head and grinned weakly.

"No. I heard that one coming just as I started out into the open and I let myself fall backwards."

I pulled myself to my feet again and ran in the direction Koon had taken. Seiden and I arrived almost simultaneously. I was gasping hard for breath and for the first time since D-day I felt the gnawing pain of dryness in my mouth. My palate rasped in my throat as I tried to swallow and I pulled hastily at my canteen. It felt light as I lifted it to my lips but the water, which had not been changed since D-day-minus-one, still was cold and fresh. I rinsed my mouth thoroughly before I swallowed and then I let the water seep slowly down my throat. I forced myself to be content with the one mouthful, for my supply was running low and I was not certain when I should be able to replenish it.

Both Koon and Seiden had left the crater before I was able to put the canteen back in its cover and I followed but at a slow trot, not because of indifference to danger, but because of exhaustion and I thought I never should have believed that, under fire and in danger, I should find it impossible to run any faster than this. And then I remembered D-day when I not only could not run, I could not walk but could only crawl and finally even my arms and legs gave way beneath me and I had to roll.

A terrific roar split the air and the roar continued and built up for what seemed seconds before it stopped. I looked back of me and saw that the second of the tanks had received a direct hit and it was burning furiously. I vaulted over the sandy rim of the shell hole and sat with Koon and Seiden and we said nothing for seconds, only staring at each other.

Another roar came and another but these were of a different sort and we peered over the edge cautiously and we saw that these sounds came from the same tank; its ammunition was exploding and we wondered how many of the crew were trapped. The tank blazed from end to end as if it had been made of wood instead of steel.

Below us and in the direction of the cliffs we could see the heads of a body of troops protruding from craters and foxholes and some were lying flat on the ground in plain view to us but hidden by slight knolls from the sight of the enemy ahead of them. Someone suggested that we join that outfit.

"We've been cut away from our platoon—most of them were on the other side of the tanks—and we might be able to do some good over there."

No one made an effort to move and the three of us sat back and rested but we were unable to relax and then, as if by a signal but without a spoken word or sign, we arose simultaneously and started down the hill again.

A hospital jeep stood in our path which led behind the body of troops, and to the left of it and nearer the dug-in Marines sat a truck. We dodged into a hole a few feet from the jeep and even as we sat down a shell exploded nearby.

"By God, they've sighted in on this jeep now," Koon said. "It's no use trying to join that outfit. The Japs'll be after that truck in a little while and then they'll have to move, too."

"We may be able to reach our outfit by going down a little way and turning back to the right," Seiden suggested. "There doesn't seem to be any fire in that direction."

We agreed this would be the best procedure and we ran out again into the open, this time at right angles to our last course. Our run changed to a trot and then to a walk and thus we came out on the beach only a few yards from the water's edge. The deep loose volcanic sand gripped at our feet and legs and even walking became intolerable but we pushed ahead until we came to ruts which had been dug parallel to the water line by our vehicles and we walked in the ruts and moved more quickly and easily.

We passed the body of a dead Marine lying to the right of the makeshift road and I slowed my pace to see if I knew him. The name on his jacket meant nothing to me and I could not see his face which was buried in the sand. It was impossible to tell when he had died, but it seemed likely that it had been on the first day of the invasion, for the shifting sands now covered half his head and piled up about his body. I passed by quickly.

Koon led the way and I followed and Seiden brought up the rear. The blazing tank still served as our landmark and when we had come to a point approximately straight below it, Koon turned to the right. I increased my pace and came abreast of him.

Neither of us said anything but we both watched for any sign of our platoon. The ascent was difficult because in this sector the incline was steep and the sand continued to be as deep and loose as it had been on the beach so that every step was a struggle and we breathed heavily and raspingly.

A head appeared in front of us and an arm motioned to us and we turned slightly to the left. We recognized then that the head was that of Kennedy and he sat in a hole near where we had dug in last night. With him was Boudrie, the platoon guide.

"Get under cover," we were told, "but stand by to move out any time. We are going up on the line on the right."

"What's the scoop?"

"I don't know. All I know is that we're going to pull out of this position."

I sat down and unbuckled my cartridge belt so that I could breathe more freely but I had barely settled into a comfortable position when the word came that we would move out.

The platoon leader formed us into a column of files and we started down the hill and to the right and our movement again was the sucking sand and the heavy breathing and the slap of canteens against hips and the whispering—*keep spread out keep spread outspreadout*—until we turned left and up the hill again. And thus we came to the top of the ridge and the shelling of the tank positions was a rumble which we forgot but was never quite dislodged from our minds. We halted frequently now and the word, which was unnecessary, passed for us to take cover at each stop. Ahead and to the right we could hear the fast short bursts of a machine gun and we knew it was an enemy weapon.

My squad had halted below the crest of the ridge but now we began to move over it rapidly. I followed the man in front of me, running low and fast, but when I crossed what I had thought was merely the top of a ridge I found myself on a plain which opened bare to the right. I saw ahead of me the violent downward sweep of a hand and I crashed to the ground as hard as if I had been swept down by the hand. I turned over on my left side and repeated the motion for the men behind me.

Groups of men from my platoon lay in shallow holes or flat against the ground ahead of me. Along the right was a terrace wall not more than two feet high and just below it lay a dead Marine. He was turned slightly onto his left side, his rifle across the top of the terrace and I felt he must have been hit while he was firing from behind what he considered a protecting wall. His helmet, which was uncovered, lay beside his body. A small dressing similar to those sold in the States under the trade name of Band-Aid stood out white above his right eye and I imagined that some frightened corpsman had made this ineffectual gesture of assistance before realizing the man was dead.

I saw then that the man had a well-developed goatee and mustache and I suddenly turned cold with anxiety for though I could not see the full face from the angle at which I lay, I was afraid that it was Heyden, the correspondent aboard the ship which had brought us to Iwo. My fear was heightened by the fact that his helmet was uncovered. I had seen no other Marine without this bit of camouflage, but I had seen uncovered helmets, identical to ours in other respects, on navy landing party personnel.

It was impossible, as it had been in the case of the Marine on the beach earlier in the day, to tell how long this man had been dead, but his skin had a purplish tinge and swarms of the great blue-green flies clung hungrily about his throat, forehead, and mouth.

Suddenly I was afraid to try to make any further identification and I was glad when the groups of men ahead of me began to move again.

124

The lieutenant sat in a shallow hole to the right of the dead man and as we started forward he shouted to one group after the other:

"Keep low. Move out fast and hit the deck often. Keep down. Move fast and hit the deck."

Kennedy rose in front of me and ran with great strides and I followed him but I knew as I got to my feet that I must run far before I hit the deck for no cover was in evidence and the machine gun chattered angrily as we showed ourselves and I ran under the kind of compulsion which pushed me after I hit the beach on D-day and my only thought was *run run run keep going don't stop you can't stop here*. But my run slowed to a near-walk and I flung myself desperately at what was not a hole nor a rut but an infinitesimally small indentation in the ground and I had the feeling that the machine gun was pointing at me alone. I wheezed asthmatically with my face in the ground between my encircling arms and the dust as it flew under my breath was red but, as the pounding of my temples eased, it again became the gray and black of Iwo. Without moving the upper portion of my body I pulled my right leg up and outward and dug my toes into the sand. When the firing of the machine gun broke off abruptly I pushed hard and was running even as I reached my feet.

The sprint brought me behind the protection of a benignly sturdy knoll and I lay against it and rested again. Others of the platoon who had preceded me were there and at intervals the remainder of my squad raced in, panting, and lay down.

We were becoming too crowded and the platoon guide shouted: "Spread out or they'll be putting the mortars in here too," and some of us slid around the back of the knoll and near what appeared to be a stone gateway leading toward the second airport. We spaced ourselves at intervals of five to ten yards along the ruts leading through this gateway and sat low with our backs pressing against the sides of embankments abutting what once might have been a road.

And we waited thus for the command to move forward again but none came. Behind us we heard the noise which meant that tanks were coming up and almost instinctively now we began to look for shelter against the mortar and artillery shells which we knew would begin dropping about us.

But nothing fell. Instead, a tank rumbled to a halt in the open space which we had just crossed, its turret swinging about like the head of a snake before it strikes, then it moved forward again over the low terrace wall.

A roaring burst made me hug the ground tightly but I looked up when I realized that it had a double sound. The man next to me said:

"That's the tank."

The roar came again a quick, double-blasting blam-wham, which I realized was the report of the gun and the sound of the exploding 75-millimeter shell as it burst almost immediately afterward.

I lifted my head but I ducked again quickly when a shower of rocks and dirt particles fell about me. Others with me cringed also and we looked up to find the tank had moved farther forward and was firing in the direction of a hillock to our right front. The tank had gone so far that it and the knoll and our position were in a line and the vehicle was firing directly toward us. It had moved to within a few feet of the aperture of a pillbox hidden in the high ground, and systematically

126

and without hurry it was pouring shells into the opening. The hillock was of sufficient height to protect us from the tank's shells or their fragments unless they went completely through the knoll; the sand and the few rocks which flew from the sides could do little, if any, damage. We settled back to comparative security, feeling good to see the tanks at last handing it out instead of taking it.

From somewhere in the rear, food and water were brought up. The water was contained in cans almost identical to those which are used for gasoline and the first man to drink complained that it tasted of gasoline. Both of my canteens were almost empty, but each of them had a small amount of water yet. My belief that I could get by with little water had proved itself true and I decided that, under normal circumstances, slightly less than one canteen would suffice me for a day. I therefore poured the water from one canteen into the other and filled the emptied container with the new water. If I were lucky I could exist on my old supply until better tasting water were brought up tomorrow. That which was tainted I could save for an emergency.

The chow was the 10-in-1 ration which contained food sufficient for one meal for ten men. It is packed in a box which, in turn, contains two packages each holding five rations. Most troops concede that 10-in-1 is the best of all field rations, but some of the choicest food items must be cooked and here no fire could be lighted.

We tore the box open, however, for most of us could have eaten anything, even if it were raw. But before we could eat there came the cry:

"Stand by for a counterattack!"

The call came from officers who had pushed ahead through the gate into the open field where the taxiway

127

ran and almost without orders we spread ourselves behind the high ground overlooking this area. We flattened ourselves, dug our toes into the sand, and squinted along the sights of our rifles but saw nothing. We saw nothing, that is, until someone sighted to our left front where, across the open ground for 200 yards, men were lying on the ground and digging in. And we swung our rifles toward them until someone raised the warning cry:

"Don't fire in that direction. That's the Twenty-fourth moving up."

A machine gun set up to the right of our platoon chattered fretfully but its fire was directed to the front and not to the left in the direction of the Twenty-fourth's lines and Beeson, who lay beside me, said:

"Look at 'em run!"

For a few seconds I saw nothing and then far across the level ground ahead of me and on the crest of a long low line of hills I could discern figures running along the ridge. They were not coming in our direction but suddenly, and for the first time since I had come on the island, anger took hold of me and I aimed at the nearest of the distant figures. Then I lifted my sights until I was aiming above the man's head and what I took to be two body widths ahead of him and I fired and the recoil made the sand run downhill in little streams from my elbows. I sighted in again as before and fired a second shot.

Beeson looked at me and it was easy to see he was barely controlling his impatience.

"I wouldn't fire at them, if I were you. You couldn't hit them at this distance, but you might draw mortar fire on our position."

"I guess you're right. I knew when I fired that I

didn't have much chance to hit anything, but I just got pissed off.''

And our vigil against a counterattack passed, for me, into the anticlimax of a gentle reading-off which I deserved and after all I did not resent it for I had fired two rounds at the Japanese and this was my first offensive action of the war.

10

It rained again that afternoon and we dug in at night only a few yards from where we had deployed to halt the counterattack which did not materialize.

We were wet and cold and hungry for we had not had a chance to eat our 10-in-1 rations. And we were mystified also, for our own push had not continued after the threat of counterattack. This was the third day of our invasion, the day on which many had said—Middleditch among them—we should secure the island. Under the official schedule we had two more days to go through to the end of the island but as yet we had not reached the 0–1 line which was the imaginary point marking termination of the first phase of the battle. After that we should be faced with the task of going to the 0–2 line which would signal the end of the second phase—in this case the capture of approximately two-thirds of the island.

I had this in mind, then, when I asked a sergeant who was a veteran of all campaigns of the Fourth Division:

"How long do you think it'll take us to secure the island, now?"

"I'd guess that it'll be at least two weeks," he said, "if we keep on as we're going now. It used to be that we made a push every day, but I don't know what's up now. It looks more like we're using army tactics than Marine Corps. We're taking it mighty slow but maybe they're trying to hold down the casualties."

I was dismayed for I trusted the sergeant's judgment and I had had no other campaign experience on which to base a disputant theory, which I sorely wanted. And like a hypochondriac I tried others whom I believed competent judges, in an effort to obtain a diagnosis which would please me more. I succeeded, for these men, like me, refused to punish themselves with realities. They lifted my morale by saying that the campaign would hardly last more than five more days, after which would come the comparatively easy job of mopping up the disorganized enemy resistance.

When we prepared our lines for the night a Japanese machine gun in the hills to our front was firing spasmodically. Beeson, with whom I was to share the foxhole, and I took turns furiously spading the soft ground, while the one who was not spading sat in a shallow communications trench to the left of our position. Our task was not too difficult and for the first time since the invasion had begun we were dug in before nightfall.

Our platoon went in small details for rations, and I wondered what had become of the box of 10-in-1's and guessed that it must have been abandoned in the heat of our defense efforts. This time we drew C rations which meant that each man would receive two cans, one containing a meat dish—usually in the form of a stew or hash or mixed with beans—and the other containing biscuits, a beverage powder and candy. We

132

also drew hand and rifle grenades and bandoliers of rifle ammunition and we staggered back from the company dump near the command post, walking parallel to our front lines and taking advantage of every shell hole along the way as a rest haven.

And now we were so tired that we slumped in our foxholes and rested before we started eating, for our exhaustion had dulled our appetites which had been on edge during the morning and early afternoon. But when we ate, the food tasted good and we consumed it with a growing appetite. I again used the blade of my combat knife as a combination fork and spoon, dishing up my beef and vegetable stew and, then, after wiping the blade clean on my dungaree trouser leg, mixed my chocolate powders in half a canteen of the gasoline-tainted water. Life was good and the cigarette which I smoked after the meal was as satisfying as is usually my first one of the day.

But work was not over, for Beeson in exploring the terrain before our hole had found the body of a Japanese soldier lying in a shallow ditch which paralleled our lines. He crawled through the communications trench in which we had taken refuge earlier and made certain the enemy soldier was dead. He brought back the man's weapon, a new rifle so little used that the yellow stock was almost unsoiled. Beeson unloaded the piece and buried the bullets in the sand and he removed the bolt and threw it as far as he could. He then tossed the now useless rifle out of the foxhole and grinned.

"That's one weapon they'll never use against us again."

As usual our lines consisted of a series of foxholes containing riflemen and BAR-men, with machine gun positions interspersed at strategic intervals along the line. On two previous nights the machine gunners had brought into the line the same .30-caliber light weapons, our chief offensive pieces, which they carried during the daytime. But tonight the word was passed that the heavier .30-caliber water-cooled guns had been brought up. They were a better defensive weapon than the lights and would be manned by machine gun crews, and the other guns would be distributed along the line to be manned by riflemen.

Because of Beeson's previous experience with the weapons, we were asked to take one of the lights into our hole and we trudged again to the company c.p. in the growing dusk to get it but now our feeling of comfort, which had come after the chow, was gone, and we were nettled for before we began our trip we had been given a lecture which we considered needless.

"You will fire," we had been cautioned, "only when it is absolutely necessary. You will not shoot at single Japs—or twos or threes or fours or fives—but only in case there really is an all-out attack. You will hold your fire," our adviser reiterated, "until you *have* to fire. The Japs want to find out where the machine guns in our lines are."

This advice, we felt, was a reflection on our common sense and Beeson replied angrily that he knew how and when to fire a machine gun. After that our anger changed to glumness and shortness with each other, and our return trip with the gun was silent and morose.

When we returned Beeson prepared an emplacement for the gun in front of our hole so that we could get grazing fire along an angle of about ninety degrees to our front. He removed the traversing bar so that the

134

weapon could be fired freely and quickly over the entire area and he inserted a belt of ammunition and cocked the weapon twice so that it was ready to be fired with a touch of the finger on the trigger.

It was completely dark now except when the yellow of the flares punctured the blackness and we sat, silent and cold, with my poncho thrown over us while we smoked a cigarette. The enemy mortar fire which seemed to rise to crescendo in the late afternoon had died away and our own artillery and mortars were laying down an intermittent barrage ahead of us. When Beeson said he would take the first watch, I pulled the poncho over my shoulders and lay down to sleep but our hole was not quite long enough to allow me to stretch out so that when my helmet touched the end a cascade of sand poured over it and over the side of my face and filled my ear. I sat up in disgust and dug at my ear with my finger but I realized I was only packing the sand tighter and I turned my head to the other side and pounded it as would a swimmer whose ears are full of water.

The motion stirred us to talkativeness and Beeson, refreshingly confident in our arms, spoke of other campaigns. He had a fierce hatred of the Japanese and he would have welcomed a full-scale counterattack that night so that we could have used the machine gun. His voice was almost caressing as he spoke of the possibility of a *banzai* charge.

But because we were both exhausted our talk petered out and I lay down again, this time carefully covering my head as well as my body with my poncho. I fell asleep almost immediately and I had difficulty in waking when Beeson shook my shoulder. I took over

135

his position at the front of the hole and he lay down under the poncho and the change of positions was made without comment.

Our hole was on a tiny rise in the ground. Directly in front of us and about fifty yards away was a knoll about ten feet high and thirty yards wide. On both sides of the knoll were shallow draws, each of which came toward and then paralleled our position in such a way that we could not see the full approach to us. But the holes to the left and right of us were placed so that their occupants, in addition to watching the level ground out front, could see down the draws. I passed my hour on watch examining the knoll and the level ground on either side of it as far as I could look. I had seen nothing when my time was up and I awakened Beeson.

Again, as on last night, when Beeson clutched and shook my leg I had the feeling that I had gone to sleep on watch and I started violently. I was wide awake when I heard him call softly to the hole on the right:

"Pass the word to stand by for a counterattack."

He paused. There was no answer.

"Pass the word to stand by for a counterattack." His voice was slightly louder.

Silence.

"God damn it over there: either answer me or pass the word."

He swore long and softly when he heard nothing and he vaulted over the parapet. He ran to the edge of the hole on the right and stood there and his voice roared suddenly and shatteringly.

"What the hell do you mean by going to sleep? Wake up, God damn you; you're supposed to be watching out front."

136

A helmeted head popped up out of the hole.

Beeson continued to shout.

"Stand by for a counterattack, do you hear? Stand by for a counterattack. Now pass the word to the right."

It was unnecessary, for anyone within fifty yards could have heard Beeson plainly but the head passed the word along and I could hear it moving haltingly up the line again.

Beeson turned on his heel and headed back toward our line, but once again he stopped.

"And let me tell you something: the next time I find all three of you asleep again I'm going to throw a grenade in that hole myself. And don't think I won't!"

He stepped into our hole and sat down. He was breathing hard in his anger and we were silent for a few moments, but the incident worried him and he pointed out the danger of our position from the draw approaching from the left because its full length could be seen only by the occupants of the hole on the right and he repeated to me his threat to throw a grenade the next time he found the three men asleep at the same time.

"There are three of them and that means with one man watching and two asleep each of them can get twice as much sleep as we can. Still if they were so tired that they fell asleep sitting up on watch, there might be some excuse, but when all three of them are lying side by side neatly covered with their ponchos . . . God damn it, they'd better watch out."

Our artillery barrage stepped up and now became steady and violent, and the flames raced up and down through the open field past our little knoll and up and over the wooded ridge in the distance. The enemy guns replied, but they weren't shelling our lines in strength.

Most of the missiles sizzled far overhead, and down on the beach an explosion became a glow and then burst with a mighty roar into towering flames and it was evident that an ammunition dump had been struck. The violent firing continued for several minutes but finally deteriorated into an occasional sibilant and thump and the flares increased in number so that the night was bright. The counterattack had not come. Beeson put his rifle carefully away and went to sleep.

My watch passed peacefully and his must have, also, for I slept the full hour. But I was not refreshed when I awoke and I watched numbly as the flares continued to arch overhead and I had to fight the sleep which clutched at my eyelids. But I was shocked into awareness when I heard the whisper approaching on my left:

"Standbystandby . . . mechanized . . ." until it came close and became "stand by for a mechanized counterattack."

I clutched Beeson's ankle hard and pulled on it. He sat up immediately. I repeated the message to him and turned to the hole on the right:

"Pass the word to stand by for a mechanized counterattack."

There was no answer.

"By God, I believe they're asleep again," I said to Beeson, and I raised my voice: "Hey, over there! Stand by for a mechanized counterattack. Pass the word along."

I kicked part of the parapet into the foxhole as I jumped out and ran to the right. The three men were as Beeson had seen them: they lay side by side, their ponchos covering them.

"Wake up, God damn it," I yelled; "we're expect-

138

ing a tank attack." One of the men stirred but did not sit up. His rifle lay on the parapet and I picked it up and struck him in the side with the butt.

He sat up hurriedly.

"Wake up and stay awake," I repeated, shouting. "There's an alert for a tank counterattack. Pass it along. You'd better stay awake, now. The next time someone's going to get hurt."

I returned to my hole and Beeson and I renewed our watch but again nothing came into view. Far up to the right a machine gun spat out a few rounds and nearer there was the light ping-whine of a Japanese grenade burst and we heard the cry of "Corpsman! Corpsman!" A few rifles along the line fired in what seemed an aimless fashion and then all was quiet except for the pop of the exploding flares. The counterattack alert died, as did so many others and we knew that the scare had arisen when someone, probably in a distant sector, had seen what he believed a dangerous concentration or unusual activity of enemy personnel or equipment.

Beeson lay down to complete his sleep and the night wore on.

11

The coldness held on even with the coming of the day which seemed to come slower now than usual. Dawn here did not seem the hesitant, almost sacred event that it was at home. Heretofore there had been only the first graying of the skies in the east and then the light rushed at you with terrifying speed. But today the grayness only thinned out across the heavens and the light grew more general but not more intense.

We were almost glad, therefore, when the call, "Stand by to move out in half an hour" provided the need for motion. The foxholes stirred and the occupants stood upright and stretched and stared about and nodded but said little.

Beeson unloaded the machine gun and put the ammunition in its box and he and I carried the equipment back to the command post. Our return trip was hurried for the half hour must have been up but as yet there was no evidence in our sector of any push forward. We sat in our foxholes and the hurried expectant seconds became uncertain minutes and the minutes grew into miserable hours which stalked before us forbiddingly.

Then it began to rain and when it became evident that we were planning no immediate advance Beeson left our hole and went to the shelter on the left to talk with Kennedy and Koon. I unrolled my poncho which I had attached to my cartridge belt preparatory to moving out and I also shed my gear again. I spread the poncho over me, wrapping it about my shoulders in such a way that when I held my rifle between my bent knees it was protected from the rain. But I had already become damp and to the dampness clung the everlasting sand and it transferred to my Garand (M-1, we called the rifle), fouling the all-important operating rod and bolt. I thought longingly of the rifle cover which I had left on board the amphibious tractor, but lacking it I removed the protective body cover from my gas mask carrier and pulled it over the rifle which I now propped in a corner of the foxhole.

Back of the line, hunched over against the rain and cold, walked Jack West. One side of his face was bloody and I asked him, with startled concern, where he had been hit. He pointed and said, "In the side of the nose," and my concern vanished and I laughed, for on the ship coming to Iwo I had reread *Cyrano de Bergerac* and West and I had heckled each other about noses and predicted dire things for one another where they were concerned. But West did not think now that being shot in the nose was funny, and of course it wasn't. Instead, he said:

"They're sending me back to the beach for treatment."

He continued to walk in the direction of the command post and although neither he nor we knew it, he had walked out of action, for, fearful of infections, physicians were allowing no casualties to return to the

142

island once they were evacuated unless their wounds had healed completely. So it was that on the fourth day, our squad had lost more than half its personnel: only six men remained: Kennedy, Koon, Beeson, Seiden, Laramie, and I.

The drizzling rain increased to a steady fall and then to a downpour and I draped the poncho over my head, and lay with my back against the crumbling sand of the side of the foxhole and the rain cover protected the front of my body completely.

I was cold and shivered as I had done each night since I had been on the island, and under the poncho I lighted a cigarette for the warmth it would bring. I saw then that my finger tips were blue and they were wrinkled as if they had been immersed overlong in water. The cigarette helped and I lighted another from it, but the second one did not taste as good and before I had finished it I snuffed it out in the sand by my side.

I noticed that the rain was soaking into the deep sand. It was not running down beneath my poncho so I relaxed and put my head back, unfastened the chin strap of my helmet and pulled the metal head cover down over my face. In this position I fell asleep.

When I awoke I had no idea of the time but I felt that I must have slept at least an hour. I was cold and shivering and when I moved, my dungarees clung clammily to me. I was wet; completely wet, except along my back. The poncho had been of little help against the rain which was still driving down.

I removed my helmet long enough to put on the poncho and snap up the sides, and then I stood up. I could see the heads of men in Kennedy's and Koon's hole and I walked over and sat with them. We talked over our casualties and they told me that Updegrave,

143

the platoon sergeant, and Matchunis, my friend from Richmond who was the runner, had been hit—Matchunis' luck had played out—but they were uncertain of the condition of either. And as we sat there the word came that a detail was needed to get chow for the platoon.

"You don't mean that we are going to get noon chow today!" I exclaimed.

"Do you know what time it is?" Koon asked.

"I'd say about twelve or one o'clock."

"It's after four."

I stood up to help carry the food and the detail formed. We walked single-file back of the lines in the direction of the command post and other men joined us to help carry ammunition and wire. For the first time we were going to string barbed wire in front of our positions.

Gunnery Sergeant Lewis checked against his record of survivors and carefully counted out one C ration for each person and I was astounded, for his record showed that we already had lost more than 100 men out of our company.

I shouldered my case of C rations and this afternoon it felt heavier than it had last night. I walked by myself and dropped the case into a shell hole back of our platoon area and returned to help carry the wire. The wire was of the type known as concertina. It is made by wrapping a single strand around an uneven number of posts stuck upright in the ground so that they form a rough circle about four feet in diameter. The wire is stapled together at every second post and the entire coil is lashed on opposite sides so that it can be carried conveniently by two men. When it is ready for use the coil can be carried hurriedly into place, one end anchored and the other end pulled in front of the area to be protected; it is this stretching out process which gives the concertina its name. When completed and anchored at both ends, it provides a wire barrier about three feet high. A single coil of concertina is not too difficult an obstacle to surmount if the attacker is going slowly, but attackers only thirty yards in front of our lines cannot afford to slow down to pick their way through wire. It is one of the simplest ways of being killed.

Boudrie and I together carried the wire and when we arrived, coils had been laid already to the right and the left of our platoon front. We used the lashing from our bundle to anchor it to the concertina on the right and we dragged the other end hurriedly behind the knoll which stood in front of my foxhole. As we ran, a machine gun fired from the ridge across the open terrain and we squatted under the protection of the little hill for several seconds until it died away. We had neither heard nor seen any evidence of bullets coming in our direction but we were taking no chances. The wire was heavy and we were confronted with the most difficult part of our job. The coil on the left did not reach the knoll and we had to stretch ours to meet it, moving out into the open where we could be seen by the enemy.

We worked slowly while we still were under cover of the knoll but when we reached the edge we pulled with a rush and the wire caught on tiny bushes which we had not noticed before and it stuck and we strained against it but to no avail. My poncho hung loosely in front of me and as I stepped forward I tripped and fell and lay, angry, where I had fallen. Boudrie turned toward our lines and shouted:

"Send me two more men to help with this wire."

Heads turned in our direction and we could see men talking but no one moved.

"God damn it, if you're coming, come on now," we screamed. "Don't stand around and beat your f——g gums all day about it."

Two men jumped from their foxholes and ran toward us. We explained what had held us up and they lifted the coil from the bushes. I threw my poncho back over my shoulders and we pulled the wire out until it could be joined on the left. We moved quickly back along it, evening the diameter as best as we could and pulling it so that it by-passed all shell holes; we wanted no Japs crawling under it where we would not see them.

The machine gun sputtered again and we fled, under the protection of the knoll, back to our positions.

Dark had come in an incredibly short time and when Beeson told me that we could have a machine gun in our hole again he and I set out to bring it up. The rain still fell, but now it was fine mist, and it gathered on our faces as does fog on a cold pane and formed into drops which ran irritatingly down our cheeks and our noses.

The men at the command post were undecided as to which gun we should have and we stood by talking for a few minutes. I heard my name called and Ray Marine strode down the hill toward me. We shook hands fervently as if we had not seen each other in years and grinned and patted each other on the back. The last time we had talked had been about a day and a half ago but that didn't seem to matter. Out here, a day and a half seemed like a lifetime and we knew that it could *be* a lifetime and we were happy to see each other safe.

Inevitably, because that is what all of us had on our minds, we talked of our casualties and Marine said:

"I almost got it again last night, Matty. Morgan did get it—pretty badly but he'll be all right, I think.

"We were in the same foxhole when a shell went off right in front of us. Morgan fell right over in my arms. I think if he hadn't spoken to me after he fell they might have had to carry me out of here with him. I was scared.

"You know, I was with MacPherson on D-day when he was killed. We had gone on a detail to get water and we were coming back across that ridge when the machine gun opened on us. I and another boy dropped flat on the ground but MacPherson tried to run for it and they cut him down and then sprayed him.

"And that's not all. I was at the c.p.—Morgan was there, too—the other day when Lieutenant H—— was killed. I guess you heard about that and knew that Captain Harshbarger was hit?"

"Yes," I said. "By the way, was the captain hit very badly?"

"He was hit pretty hard, I think, but I couldn't tell. He was sitting down when the shell hit and after it had landed he just sat there for a minute with his head sort of tilted to one side. Then he looked around slowly and said: 'Those yellow bastards are going to kill us all yet,' and he got up and walked off to the aid station."

The gun Beeson and I were to take was pointed out to us and we collected ammunition for it. Lieutenant D——, executive officer now that Captain Harshbarger had been wounded and Captain Helton elevated to company commander, stood nearby joking with the men.

"I guess you know," one of them said, "that this is

the fourth day of our two-day stay on the front lines.'' He was referring to shipboard scuttlebutt that we would be relieved after two days on the line, would not have to return since the campaign would require only three to five days.

"Yep," said the lieutenant, "time flies, doesn't it?"

"And," another reminded him, "how about those clean dungarees and socks they were going to bring in to us on the third day?"

"I'll tell you about those," he replied. "They were a little mussed up and had to be pressed. As soon as Major A—— finishes sewing buttons on them, he'll bring them right up."

We waited in nearby shell holes, but Lieutenant D—— disdained their shelter. He stood in the open, his hands thrust deep in his trousers pockets, his dungaree jacket collar turned up against the rain. He wore a baseball cap—as did most of his machine gun platoon—under his helmet. He was as cool under fire as he was on the parade ground. Someone later told me of the time on D-day when a member of his platoon shouted for him to get under cover.

"I wouldn't," the lieutenant answered, "give them the satisfaction of seeing me duck."

Beeson and I stood up and shouldered the weapon and ammunition boxes and struggled through the sand. Czaja walked ahead of us and he warned us to use the back route to our shelter, which meant only that we should take advantage of the shell holes a few yards back of the line rather than walk exposed along the crest where the line lay. We did and the climbing into and out of the craters with the gun, which was very difficult to carry with its heavy mount, left us weak with fatigue by the time we arrived at our position.

148

Beeson set to work with the entrenching tool again, improving the frontal position which he had scooped out hastily last night and while he worked Seiden came over and said he wanted to help operate the weapon. Because our foxhole was built to accommodate only two men, I offered to move into the hole with Kennedy and Koon, since Seiden knew more about the operation of the weapon than I did.

He and I exchanged places and I moved to the hole on the left and slumped into the bottom. Kennedy and Koon had started on their chow and I joined them, attacking my meat and beans with the combat knife which was gritty with wet sand. The rain fell more heavily now and we shivered as we ate. We buried our empty cans, sharp edges down, and covered the bottoms with sand to prevent light reflections. Koon and I covered ourselves with a poncho and Kennedy lay down under another and fell into an exhausted sleep. He had been feeling badly, Koon explained, a fact which was easy to see. He had fallen asleep with gum in his mouth and in his sleep he chewed on it and occasionally his teeth would grate together harshly and his muscles trembled continuously in a violent shiver which shook the poncho lying over him.

Koon and I were shivering too and we cursed the rain and the cold wind which blew it into our faces and we agreed that neither of us had ever been more miserable, and the confession of our misery made us more uncomfortable than ever.

Off to the left we heard a whisper and we knew someone was trying to attract our attention. We thrust our heads up and saw Boudrie, now acting platoon sergeant, half running, half crawling in our direction. He thrust a bottle into our foxhole.

"Here, take a slug of this," he said. "But hurry; I want to pass it around to all the fellows in the platoon."

"Great God!" I said. "Where'd you get this?" It was a quart of bourbon whisky.

"Ask me no questions," he grinned, "just go ahead and drink."

I pulled at the bottle and passed it to Koon and the contraction of my muscles eased almost as soon as the liquor passed into my throat. Koon drank and we woke Kennedy who, almost dazed, swallowed and lay down and slept again. We thanked Boudrie fervently and he ran toward Beeson and Seiden with the bottle.

We pulled the empty C ration box into the foxhole for use as a seat by the man on watch and Koon and I decided that we should rotate the guard between the two of us for a few hours to give Kennedy a chance to sleep and I offered, because I had slept long that day, to take the first watch. We had only two ponchos for the three of us and we agreed that the two sleepers should have the protection while the watch sat uncovered. Koon lay down but almost immediately it began to rain hard again and he arose and sat beside me and threw the poncho over both of us. When the rain ended it was time for my watch to end and he insisted that he was not sleepy now and although I knew he must be lying graciously, I lay down, pulling the poncho over me. I fell asleep at once, for I was so wet that the dampness of the ground now meant nothing to me.

When I awoke our artillery again was firing heavily into the territory ahead of us and the shrapnel flew back over our lines. I sat with my head well out of the hole so that I could see in all directions but when the

150

shell splinters flew I ducked close to the rim.

I found that night that imagination was a wonderful and terrible thing. The night before I had been worried by several bumps along the knoll ahead which could have been the heads of men. During the day I had seen that the bumps were tufts of grass and I counted them carefully—two here, one there and three there—and now I was resolved that if a seventh one appeared I should fire. And tonight I recounted the knots at regular intervals until suddenly I discovered a new mental hazard. To the right of the highest point of a knoll was a small bush and behind it I could make out, when the bush was silhouetted by the flares, the form of a squatting man. And I said to myself, no, that can't be a man; it must be the foliage. No one but a fool would squat on top of the ridge that way. But I continued to stare and the more I looked the more convinced I became that it was a man. I brought my rifle up from beside me and laid it pointing across the parapet at the knoll and I sighted down it, fingering the trigger but not releasing the safety because I wanted to be absolutely certain before I fired. My imagination began to play tricks on me and the figure moved a small shuffling step to the left. I flicked the safety catch off with my right forefinger and aimed again, this time prepared to fire. But a flare which had opened late fell, still burning brightly, directly behind the knoll, and through the image of my "man" I could see the gleam of light. It was foliage. I pressed the safety catch into the trigger guard again.

The dawn of the fifth day was cold and gray and the sun apparently had lost its way but we had a rumor which was better than the sunlight. We were going to be relieved! Despite our misery we were almost hilarious when we heard it and although we knew it couldn't be true our need for some optimism forced us to believe it. But it was true.

The relief, members of the Twenty-fourth Marines, came onto the line during a Japanese mortar and artillery barrage. Just before they straggled into view a five-inch shell landed only a few yards back of our hole. It was a dud. But the morning turned beautiful even under the clouds and then the clouds themselves broke and the sun shone through.

We stood up in our shelters and called gaily to each other and we magnamimously left for our successors on the line our grenades and extra bandoliers of ammunition which had weighted down not only our bodies but our spirits and we walked in a single file down from the line and toward the rest area. Our leaders had to order us to take cover as we moved and our freed spirits were nettled so that when the leaders were not looking we straightened up and walked disdainfully. And I was walking thus when I felt a blow on my back, my knees buckled and I sprawled forward. I knew I was hit but also knew immediately that whatever had hit me had not penetrated the skin. I raised myself to my knees and looked about. Embedded in the sand behind me was a large piece of shrapnel. I picked it up and it burned my hand and I thrust it into a pocket. It had struck me with the force of a hard-thrown baseball and my back still stung from the impact. I loosened my cartridge belt and ran my hand under my jackets and shirt but I felt no blood and I replaced the belt and fell into line again. This time I walked cautiously and the day seemed less bright.

It was my first really close call of the operation. The

second came only a short time later. Kennedy and I dug our foxhole on a little ridge overlooking the rest area. In compliance with the orders of our officers we removed our leggings and shoes and socks and we sat together in the shelter cleaning our rifles. I had removed my helmet but our platoon leader had told me to put it back on. He had just moved away when the air roared and turned black and the ground rocked and the foxhole collapsed into itself and something wrenched me violently. Kennedy was lying across my lap and I was shaken but I knew I was unhurt.

"Are you hurt, Kennedy?" I asked.

"I don't know; I don't think so."

He wasn't and sat up again. We vaulted out of our hole and ran to a nearby shell crater and sat in it. We both were shaken and it was several minutes before we could bring ourselves to go into the open long enough to learn that a shell had struck only three feet from the edge of our shelter.

This was our rest area!

That night I slept again with my helmet on. I slept the sleep of the exhausted, secure in the knowledge that I should not have to stand watch. The only time I awoke was when my helmet rolled off my head and I was uncomfortable and put it on again.

12

Water still was not sufficient to allow the washing of faces and teeth, and cleanliness continued to be an impossible luxury. Not all the good things were denied, however.

I remember the first day back when they brought up the coffee. It was in the same kind of can which held the water and the gasoline, but it tasted like neither water nor gasoline: it tasted like coffee.

I remember, too, how we went into childish ecstasy over the sight and the smell of it and how we crowded around the cook who poured it out only an inch deep in the canteen cups when we would have liked to swim in it. We were so pleased with this, our first hot drink, that we even forgot to beat our gums about the scarcity of it.

And they brought around the so-called assault rations that day, too. Forewarned, I expected a new kind of food preparation and found, instead, that we were getting a ration of cigarettes, hard candy, chewing gum, and matches.

We ate hot food, then. It was the 10-in-1 ration and

we built tiny fires of composition C-2, the powerful explosive from the demolition man's kit, and fed them with the tarred paper from the 10-in-1 ration container and with splintered wood from grenade cases. We cut the paper and hewed the wood and stirred the food and ate it—each man did all this with his combat knife. We poured water from our canteens into our canteen cups and ringed the fire with the cups until the water was hot and we made joe and hot chocolate from powders and although we burned our lips on the cups it still was good.

The bacon came in large cans which we opened and set in the center of the flames, along with the English stew, and we ate out of the community can. It was primitive, perhaps, but to us it was a good way of life. We liked the 10-in-1 ration—not only because it gave us a balanced meal; it contained the niceties, too, like sugar and butter and canned milk. And toilet paper. And many of us attended to personal matters which we had neglected since D-day. A centrally located shell hole served as a head and each man who visited it went not only with the new toilet paper but with his entrenching tool. Ever mindful of the dangers of dysentery, we dug deep holes into which we voided and which we then refilled with sand. This, too, was primitive, but it was better than the arrangements some men had to make on the line when they were pinned in their shelters by enemy fire and were compelled to dig into one end of the foxholes in which they later were to sleep.

We were allowed to order all manner of new things from the quartermaster: dungarees, shoes, socks, underwear, rifle cleaning equipment—even, in the case of some, rifles. And, although the only result of this ordering was the issuance of one new pair of cotton socks to each man, the gesture was pleasant.

The overworked corpsman received little rest because, having no new wounded to treat, he now had time to minister to the rest of us, and we went to him with all our ailments. One member of our platoon, who had a fever, was evacuated to a hospital ship; for most of us he merely painted our feet which were turning white and soft and cracking with the beginning of trench foot. Then most of us again donned our filthy, still-wet socks, for we had thrown away or used as rifle cleaning rags the unserviceable cottons which we had just received.

As an afterthought I asked Scala to look at my right thumb which was slightly sore and red along the end of the nail. There was little to be seen, however, and he swabbed it with a red solution and I left his temporary aid station, having dismissed the matter from my mind.

Our proximity to the front lines and the certainty that we were under observation made dangerous any large gatherings, but we were together enough for a sense of release, and now laughter and conversation no longer seemed obscene.

But beyond all the other delights was that of sleeping. We maintained only one guard post at night, manned by two men at a time. I was assigned to stand the watch for two hours with Beeson, but Koon, who slept with Beeson, asked me to change places on the guard with him. Let him go tonight, he said, and I could take his place the next time. (The following night all of us stood watch; we were back on the line.)

Not even an air raid—our first of the operation—halted sleep. It merely delayed it for a short time.

Shortly after dark we were warned to stand by for "condition red"—the raid warning. Far off in the direction of the beach we could hear a loudspeaker giving directions of action to be taken in case enemy planes came overhead. Condition red had been announced the night before, but no planes had appeared. Tonight the Japs came over.

Far off in the distance we heard the hum of an airplane engine but we did not know it was Japanese until a lone 20-millimeter gun on a warship pumped a few hesitant red tracers into the sky and suddenly the air turned into a vast inverted funnel of sparks as thousands upon countless thousands of rounds of ammunition were hurled at the Japanese and the ground trembled under the impact of the sound from the ships. And over that sound could be heard the dull crump . . . crump . . . crump-crump-crump of bombs exploding somewhere. The firing died away and built itself up as the plane turned back over the island from the sea or new ones appeared. In the light of the tracers we had seen only one plane, but surely such a reception would have been reserved for more formidable visitors.

Kennedy and I lay on our backs in the foxhole and looked at the spectacle above, awed by the splendor, and it was not until the raid was over that someone came by our shelter and said:

"You'd better sit up as straight as you can without exposing your heads during an air raid. Lying down that way, you might get all cut up by falling flak. But if you sit up and keep your head down your helmet will deflect most of the stuff from your body and the only things which will stand much chance of getting hit are your shoulders and legs."

With which happy thought he left us, wondering whether some errant bit of flak might be waiting to pounce on us at this late hour.

By the next day we felt well at home in the rest area and we began paying calls on our neighbors who were members of Able and Baker companies in our battalion.

It was John H——, of Able, who told me of the young lieutenant who had bawled and profaned us through the advanced training at Camp Lejeune. This lieutenant, it seemed, had set himself up in the hearts of his men forever by coming onto the beach and attacking, single-handed, three Japs in a foxhole. According to H—— he shot two of the enemy soldiers and beat the third to death with the butt of his carbine which he shattered in the attack.

I returned from visiting H—— to find Eddie L——, who also went through Camp Lejeune with me, waiting to see me. L—— always had considered himself a man of considerable experience with women and he talked a triumphant seduction.

Today he said:

"Matty—never more! The next war I stay home. I really think I ought to go home right now. I'm no fighting man; I'm much better in bed than in battle."

Despite his attempt at humor, he was visibly shaken. His company had been thrown against the cliffs on our right flank and it had been cut up badly as it beat its way to the crest. He, like the rest of us, was full of his experiences and the two of us bored each other with vivid but obvious lies about our close calls in battle.

L—— returned to his company area and a short time later we were told to stand by to move out.

159

We walked down from the rest area in the direction of the cliff and as we went our leaders whipped us into a semblance of a GI advance—a staggered, scattered column of files which changed into a skirmish line when we turned right toward the beach, and a column of files again when we faced left toward the cliff. But we didn't take the maneuvering too seriously for yesterday we had seen the orange front line panels atop the cliff, which meant that it was ours, and we could see the troops dodging and running and crawling toward the ridges back of the cliff. We felt comparatively safe and we walked carelessly although we were under direct orders to move fast and low and when we halted we went through the motions of seeking safety in nearby shell holes but we usually sat on the rims rather than deep within them as we should have, had we felt the need for caution.

At our last turn toward the cliff we moved along the road down which Koon and Seiden and I had plunged in escaping the mortar barrage three days earlier. Dusk had camouflaged the area in a monotonous gray when we halted at the foot of the cliff and our squad squatted on their heels at the edge of a combination command post and aid station. A few yards away the radio in a jeep moaned out the notes of a recording of ''Begin the Beguine,'' and a clarinet wailed up over the subdued talk of the men. But we stirred restlessly for the area had an oppressive odor and someone pointed out the body of an enemy soldier, badly torn by shrapnel, lying on the edge of a nearby shell crater, and almost at once we saw in front of us a group of stretchers, each bearing a Marine and the faces of all these men were covered with blankets. They were dead also and I saw that on the stretcher nearest me the blanket lay flat

160

from the occupant's hips down and I wondered how the man had lived long enough to be brought to the aid station.

We moved quickly and cautiously after that for our mood of security was gone, and our tempers frayed rapidly. We struggled up the face of the cliff along a tiny path which, despite its size, must have been the main thoroughfare for our advancing troops and we cursed and grumbled in low voices as we tripped over tiny communications wires which meshed along the path. However, our talk and even our curses died suddenly when the cliff path rose steeply and before we had arrived at the crest we were exhausted and our breath came in small gasping wheezes. We did not stop to rest because from the shadows of a ridge ahead came a soft call:

"Joe! Joe! Move your men this way."

And another voice, strident, loud, urgent:

"And for the love of Christ get a move on."

We crossed the ridge and halted abruptly and we were dispersed in groups of three and four men and told to dig in. Officers scuttled from group to group and gave us the scoop. We were, they said, in reserve. The front line lay about 200 yards ahead of us and our main purpose was to protect the rear of this line. Our own positions lay across the main evacuation route and we could expect, they continued, to see wounded men coming back from our front and the Japs might try to slip men through us by the same route. For this reason we must challenge everyone we saw. Now dig in—here and here and here, and they pointed to the specific places where they wanted the holes to be. Our squad was at the left end of the line and the point at which Koon and Beeson and Laramie dug anchored

161

the flank and overlooked a small valley which fell away from other ridges ahead. Our spot was approximately five yards away to the right of them and slightly forward and our rear was marked by the shattered trunks of two trees.

We removed our entrenching tools from their carriers and fell to work in the dark but we had cleared away no more than six inches of soil when we began to run into huge rocks which struck sparks off our entrenching tools as we swung them. And although the night again was cold we removed our combat and dungaree jackets as we worked and we abused the situation and the names of the men who had put us in it. The rocks were not our only obstacles, for growing around and clinging to them were large roots of the trees. Lieutenant D——, the executive officer, walked by and we complained to him that we were unable to put a hole in this position. He looked about for an instant, saw no other likely location, and said sarcastically:

"Well, you people just step back a little and I'll call on the artillery to blow you a hole."

We fell to work again and we used the stones from the hole as our parapet and our entrenching tools did double duty as we hacked at the roots but we gave up when we were a foot below the surface, considering our position now safe enough. We donned our jackets again and sat in the shelter and it was not until then that we discovered that our hole was useless. Directly ahead of it was the stump of a tree out of the base of which grew foliage so low that we had not noticed it as we stooped or stood in the hole, but it was so thick that a sitting watcher could not see ahead of our position. Flanking the stump were small bushes which further obscured our vision.

"We won't be able to see a damn thing."

"A Jap'd be able to crawl right in our laps before we could see him."

"Yeh, they could grenade us silly and we wouldn't know what hit us."

"We need a fire lane out front."

"You ain't kiddin'."

"Well—*something* ought to be done."

"Uh-huh."

We sat without moving.

"Oh, Christ! we aren't getting anywhere sitting here like this. We've got to do something about it so we might as well get started."

We hauled our protesting bodies erect and ran in front of our shelter. With our entrenching tools and combat knives we hacked and cut at the underbrush for several yards.

"I think that'll be all right," Kennedy said and we returned to our shelter. It was better and now we had fairly clear terrain ahead except for a small blind spot beyond the tree stump which we had been unable to destroy. We huddled low and discussed the watch situation and it was decided that, since we were in reserve, only one man need be on guard at a time. This would allow each of us to get two hours of sleep for each hour of watch. But it did not work out that way, for we were barely through with the discussion before a grenade popped to the left and the shrapnel whined but hit short of us. Another burst followed.

Thus for a time at least the guard became a matter for all three of us; it was evident that Japs were between us and the front line. On the left we could see the heads of Koon, Beeson, and Laramie, craning to peer in the direction of the grenade explosions, and behind us a voice called out softly to us. It was Gunnery Sergeant Lewis and he walked up to our hole, looking top-heavy in a fleece-lined navy jacket. He carried a carbine in his right hand.

"That valley," he nodded in the direction from which had come the sounds of the grenade, "is lousy with Gooks. Two or three of us are going out to do some hunting. For God's sake don't fire out in that direction until we give you the word or you see something you *know* is a Jap."

We assured him we'd hold our fire, but we pointed out that we weren't on the flank and he walked to the hole on our left and repeated his warning and then disappeared back of us below the ridge we had climbed earlier.

Soon calm descended over our sector and we began the rotation of our watch. Ahead of us we could hear the sound of enemy mortar and artillery shells landing in or close to our front line and occasionally to our left front we could see the flashes of our own mortars being fired and hear the s-s-s-s-chunk-s-s-s-s-chunk . . . chunk-chunk-s-s-s-s.

And then bedlam broke loose about our mortar positions and we could hear the shouts of the men and the sharp fiery cracks of carbines being fired rapidly and in the night and at a distance of approximately 150 yards, they sounded like toys in comparison with the authoritatively blunt M-1. But the tumultuous outburst faded to the sporadic punctuation of a single carbine and then slowly died away entirely.

We knew then that the Japanese had infiltrated through the front line or else they had stayed under cover as our troops advanced past their positions during the day, attacking under cover of darkness in an

164

effort to wipe out the mortar section. How well they succeeded we had no way of knowing.

But to our left a rifle barked flatly and I looked at the next hole and saw Beeson with his weapon still at his shoulder. It was pointed into the valley at his left. One of the other men with him knelt briefly at his side and spoke a few words to him and then lay down again but Beeson remained fixed behind the sights on his rifle. I looked carefully over the land in front of me but saw nothing and I looked again at the adjoining shelter. Beeson continued to hold his aim at a point in the valley. He had not moved when the hour was ended and it was time to change the watch, but when his successor sat up beside him he relaxed and pointed in the direction toward which he had fired.

I, too, was relieved and I fell asleep and sometime between my falling asleep and my being roused for my next watch I stirred and recognized the sound of rifle fire but I did not awaken fully. And later in the night I again was conscious of shooting somewhere along the line without really awakening. We actually were awake only during the time for our watches but we never slept soundly for we had so schooled ourselves to listen always that every sound struck through our sleep and was assimilated by us. But the sounds of shooting and of explosions were also commonplace now and only the sound of a voice—a rare thing at night— interrupted our half-sleep.

The day had barely begun to break when I awoke. Up and down our sector men were moving about and as the day brightened their speech returned and they shouted to one another as they moved about. I walked over to Beeson's hole and he told me that he had fired the night before at a Jap in the valley and he knew that he had missed and the Jap flattened himself in the grass where he could not be seen. Beeson had kept his aim on the spot where the enemy soldier fell but for half an hour he had seen no movement. He had tried to point out to his successor where the man lay but the Marine had confused the position so that when the Jap made a sudden sprint for safety he had fired too late.

Seiden, beaming, joined us and displayed a small wrist watch he had taken from the body of a Japanese ahead of our lines. It was a small steel instrument enclosed in a larger weather-proof casing. I admired it and he said:

"You ought to see the one Degliequi got. It's a combination regular pocket watch and stop watch and a beauty. He got it off a Gook he and Mikell killed last night."

That, I told myself, accounted for the second burst of firing I heard.

Degliequi was the center of a cluster of Marines when I arrived at his hole and he held out to me the watch he had taken from the victim of his shooting. It was a pocket watch and its face was intricately marked for its dual purpose. In the foxhole was Mikell, carving his name into the stock of the enemy soldier's rifle. When we moved out a short time later he carried his heavy BAR over one shoulder, his souvenir over the other.

We were back in the rest area and again scuttlebutt had it that we probably were there to stay—we had served our time on the line and a runner said he had it straight from headquarters that a push toward the 0–2 line had begun and that if it were reached by nightfall the island would be secured in two more days.

166

But we cleaned our weapons diligently anyhow and we fired them and most of them failed to work semiautomatically and had to be recleaned and then cleaned again and even then the rust spots still showed dully from beneath the coat of oil.

We knew something big must be brewing, for, from the direction of the beach, men poured through our rest area toward the front lines almost unceasingly and we talked to them or waved to them or heckled them and we were amazed and nettled when some of them said they had not been on the line in five days.

Turlo, the squad leader, rejoined us later that afternoon and he grinned triumphantly as we slapped him on the back and shook his hand. He declared the doctor had said his wound was not healed sufficiently for him to be allowed to return to the island, but he had sneaked into a small boat leaving the transport on which he had been treated and had come despite the physician. He talked with us briefly and then set about replacing his weapons and gear which he had lost in being evacuated.

Others joined us also that afternoon. They were replacements and it was clear that the scuttlebutt had been wrong for we knew they wouldn't replace an outfit which was to remain in rest area. The new men were assigned to the squads of which they would be members and they huddled together in shell holes, uncomfortable in their anticipation of combat.

And the order came for us to stand by to move out before dawn.

13

When we reached the line, the men in the foxholes seemed startled to see us, but they were wordless as they clambered out into the open and walked toward the rear. We took their places in the line.

The boy with me, a replacement whom I had never seen before, looked steadily at the ground. He stooped and picked up a box of K ration, stripped it open and removed the chewing gum. He offered me the other contents of the box. I took the package of cigarettes and started to throw the rest away but I reconsidered, opened and ate the can of pork and egg yolks.

"This," said the boy, "is a hell of a way to spend a birthday."

"This your birthday?"

"Yeh."

"How old are you?"

"Nineteen."

We were silent and I thought it *is* a hell of a way to spend a birthday, especially a nineteenth birthday. The boy looked pitifully young with his load of gear and the strain that already marked his face.

"It usually rains on my birthday," he said, still looking at the ground. I looked at the sky and saw that it was cloudy.

"It rained the day I was born. So they tell me. And it usually rains every birthday." He sounded irritated by the thought. "It rained last year and the year before and—oh, nearly every year that I can remember."

"Well, it looks as if it may rain today. That ought to make it official," I said.

"Yeh," he brightened. "I wouldn't hardly know what to do unless it rained on my birthday."

Our artillery fire went on overhead in a continuous sizzle, bursting in loud, ugly rumbles in the distance.

I heard my name called and peered over the side. It was Turlo.

"Stand by to push off," he shouted and I repeated his words to the hole on my right. Almost immediately I heard from my left:

"Let's move out."

I picked up my rifle and put one foot on the edge of the foxhole and stepped up. The sand crumbled under my weight and I half fell, then crawled onto more solid ground. I stood up and looked about. I did not know in what direction we were going to move.

"Where's our front?" I shouted at Turlo and he waved slightly to the right of the position I faced.

A handful of Marines now stood about their shelters, diffident and nervous, waiting for someone else to start the push. They shuffled their feet and looked at their rifles or at the ground and many of them stood with their backs to the direction in which the attack would go.

"Well, let's move," an officer called and his shout rose to an angry scream. "God damn it, are you people

170

going to move out or are you going to sit there all day?"

I fell in with my squad and we formed a skirmish line with other outfits which stretched as far as I could see to the right and the left and we walked slowly away from our line onto a down grade and the calls rose about us, "Don't crowd up—spread out, spread out. Don't crowd up. God damn it, keep a good interval in there," and "Move to the right, over there; move to the right," and the faces of the men about me were strained and I thought my face must look the same. We crept forward, half-sidling and crouched low, our rifle butts pressed against our right hips or sides and the muzzles pointing forward and I thought irrationally this is what those months of training have built up to, for I had a sense of foreboding, of impending disaster, but it was no stronger, perhaps, than I had had in previous pushes into the front line.

The rocky terrain on which we had started gave way to tall grass and the grass to a thicket of scrub palms and banyans, and my forced alertness pulled at every nerve and gripped my muscles so that they ached with the tension and I said to myself this is an ideal place for the Japs to be and they will open fire any minute. But nothing happened.

We halted in the thicket to allow our line to straighten and I knelt on one knee as low as possible and when the talking of the officers and the non-coms died away it was so eerily quiet I could hear the rapid breathing of the man on my right. And we arose and moved forward again.

Down below us the palm thicket ended and in front the ground leveled off. Beginning at each end of the tree line and swinging away from us to encompass the level ground lay a semicircular ridge and it looked forbidding and steep from our position on the hill. Our line wavered and straightened out. We moved forward steadily again, slowly and cautiously, but steadily. We could see nothing but we sensed something must be there and again the feeling of disaster built up hot in me and we passed the tree line and hunched into the open, level, unprotected ground.

A rifle cracked sharply in front of me and, even as our line scattered and I saw a Marine run forward a few steps and plunge into a hole, I heard the short quick burst of a machine gun followed immediately by a crashing of small arms fire and over the din I heard the shouts of the Marines back of me and I found myself lying in a shallow hole.

And my mind said *I knew it I knew it* and then it contradicted itself and I found myself wondering if this really could be I or if I were merely detached and looking at something happening to others but not to me. But even as I plunged into the hole I saw a puff of dirt fly from the hill in front of me and my mind registered clearly this time, for above the puff was a tiny black hole and I said *there is a pillbox don't take your eye off it you won't be able to find it again there is a pillbox* and I kept my eye on it and pulled my rifle up from my side and aimed and again my training told, for I said to myself line 'em up at six o'clock on the bull and squee-ee-eeze 'em off.

I set the black hole on top of my sights and flicked the safety mechanism with my right forefinger and squeezed the trigger and the rifle bounced up in the air. I settled my elbows firmly and fired again and then quickly twice more and the ground in front of my rifle spat dirt into the air and I ducked and something

172

stitched across the back of my shell hole. I squirmed around until I was lying parallel with the ridge. I pressed the side of my face into the sand and held my breath and pulled my legs up tight so that my heels pressed firmly against my rump and I lay there without moving for what may have been several minutes or several seconds.

I raised my head cautiously and when it was less than three inches off the ground I could see the top half of the ridge ahead of me and I knew that if I could see the top half anyone in that portion of the steep slope could see me and I buried my face in the ground again quickly.

Directly behind me I could hear the strident cry, "Corpsman! Corpsman!" and I knew someone was hit. I turned on my other side so I could look toward the rear. The machine gun chattered again violently and someone screamed:

"Get down, Scala! For God's sake get down!"

I saw Doc Scala fling himself at the ground but the machine gun continued to fire for a short time. Like haunting echoes now from the left and the right could be heard the urgent wail, "Corpsman! Corpsman!" We weren't the only platoon being hit; others were catching it, too.

To the right and rear of the place where Scala lay I could see helmets expose themselves briefly and flash back under the protecting cover of the ground and each time they showed themselves the machine guns and rifles back of me flared angrily and the bursts came and went irregularly. I twisted again so that I faced the ridge and I clung as close as I could to the front of my shelter but my position was cramped and I raised my head and looked back and I saw the helmet of a Marine behind me. The man peered up out of his hole and looked at me and then waved violently with a downward motion of his hand. I resumed my position, looking forward into the sand in front of my crater.

My right hip ached and I shifted my body and saw that I was lying on what appeared to be the battered pieces of a palm tree trunk but I realized that in the position in which I now lay my left hip probably could be seen from the ridge. I did not dare sit up long enough to try to pry the wood up and throw it out of the whole and I moved back so that I lay on it as before. The motion had rested the hip slightly but as I lay there the pain returned and the numbness began to creep into my toes and move slowly across the top of my foot and up my leg. I turned my body quickly so that my back and head pressed against the front wall of the shell hole and I straightened my leg as much as possible and rubbed my thigh with my right hand. The numbness turned into needle-like pricks across my foot and then they disappeared, but the numbness now had invaded my left foot. I twisted onto my right side again and I forced my weight as much as possible against my hip and felt the wood sink a little into the sand and my position became more comfortable.

But not for long. I felt a drop of water on the side of my face and another and then another and the rain came, slowly and irritatingly, and I loosened my helmet strap and slid the helmet over the left side of my face. I thought of the replacement back on the hill early this morning and I said this makes it official, all right, and I wondered if he were alive still to enjoy the satisfaction which this should bring him. But the downpour increased and my thoughts turned to my own discomfort. I buttoned the collar of my combat jacket, the left side of which was dark already from the water, and I thrust my rifle between my legs so that the operating rod and bolt were protected. The motion made my wet trousers adhere to my legs and I began to shiver.

I ached for a smoke and I reached inside my jacket and drew out a cigarette and a package of matches. I put the cigarette between my lips and then I thought this hole is so small that the smoke won't have a chance to be dispelled in the air before it rises above the surface of the ground and the Japs will be able to see it and know someone is here and they can keep me spotted by the smoke. I removed the cigarette and crushed it into the sand.

To the left I heard the shout of a voice I believed to be Seiden's and I yelled, mostly because I needed something to relieve my loneliness:

"You all right, Seiden?"

I thought I heard an affirmative answer and I called again:

"How about the rest?"

This time I heard nothing and the loneliness closed in on me again until I felt like a child alone in a dark room: I could see nothing but I felt that a thousand hostile eyes were watching me.

Suddenly I felt desperately tired and the exhaustion was accompanied by an overwhelming desire to sleep. I moved the helmet off the side of my face and let the rain fall against my skin. I screwed my legs up tightly beneath me. I thought again of a cigarette and again I discarded the idea and instead I pinched my chin and my cheeks and I listened to the sound of the machine guns rattling ahead of me and I scooped a mound of sand out of the front of my hole and spread it flat and built it up again, merely for the action it required. But the action only accentuated my exhaustion and I relaxed for an instant. I dozed.

Then my eyes jerked open. I had been roused not by a noise but by the absolute silence which tore at my consciousness. I could not hear a sound. There was no gunfire and nothing to denote the presence of life. I listened intently and then twisted rapidly in my hole so that I looked toward what had been our positions to the rear. Nothing moved and I thought *this is it; you've slept and the rest of them have pulled back* and I knew that I had been in front of our main positions and that others had probably forgotten I was there and cold fear tore at me with giant hands and I knew then also that I had never before experienced real fear. The rain had stopped and the sun was trying to break through the clouds but I shivered violently and the shivering was different from anything I had ever experienced at night for I shook not only with the muscles in my legs and arms and fingers and neck but I trembled violently internally, too, and my stomach at the base of my ribs felt as if it were suffering from a great *tic;* it was caught first in a mighty hand which squeezed so violently that my breath caught and then the spasms eased off gradually, only to clutch me angrily again. I realized, too, that my breath was coming almost by conscious effort alone and when I tried to slow the action of my lungs the attempt hurt physically.

This is how death would come. I wondered then why it could not strike swiftly and easily. A bullet through the head seemed painless alongside this; there had been no sign of pain on the faces of those I had seen who had been hit thus. I tried to rationalize death in the face of my fear and I thought of my family and that was painful. I tried to put the thought aside but could not and they were with me as clearly as if they sat there in the flesh. I knew then more keenly than I'd ever felt before that I did not want to die but I hoped that if I had to die I would go quickly. And the knowledge that my death could cause grief created in me almost a feeling of shame. I knew that was an irrational thought but it persisted.

And I thought if I only knew where the Japs were. I twisted to my right side and lifted my head so that I could see the ridge and the dust spurted angrily in front of me and I heard afterwards the almost detached light sound of the machine gun firing. I ducked again. I lay breathing heavily looking into the sand a few inches in front of my face.

But the sound of movement near the top of my hole broke in upon my consciousness and I looked up to see a land crab moving down toward me. At the time it looked tremendous but it probably was no more than three inches in diameter. I clutched my rifle with the butt toward the crab, calculated the distance and smashed at it violently but because of my cramped position I missed and it raced down the side of the hole and under my right hip. My muscles tensed and my mind cried out to move and my stomach squeezed again but I thought of the machine gun ahead of me and I lay still except for the trembling of my muscles. I saw no more of the animal nor did I feel it move after it went under me, and I relaxed slowly.

And then for the first time since I had dozed I heard the sound of a voice in the distance behind me and I twisted again to my left side and from the direction toward which my head pointed, and sounding very close, came another shout:

"Meuse! Hey, Moose!" It was the voice of Koon and it sounded high-pitched and a little unnatural. "What's the scoop?"

The answer was indistinguishable to me and I waited a few seconds before I called:

"Koon! You all right?"

"Yeh."

"Where are you? How close are you to me?"

"I don't know; I can't see you."

I held up my hand.

"I can see your hand plain; you're just a little way from us."

"How many are there with you?"

"There's just two of us here. Czaja's with me."

"You got room for any more in your hole?"

"Sure, it's a big hole. Come on over. You're just to the left of me. But be careful and get the hell over here in a hurry."

The terrible fear had gone out of me when I heard his voice and I knew with certainty that much of it came from the fear of loneliness, of being abandoned.

I gathered my feet under me again and waited briefly before I threw myself upward and over the side of the hole and the sand crumbled under my feet and I stumbled but I caught myself with my left hand and without stopping I regained my balance and plunged on upright. I saw immediately the hole and Koon and Czaja; they were only a few yards away. They watched me with concern stamped on their faces until I raced down the side of their shelter and then they grinned and motioned me to put my head down. A rifle cracked and although I did not hear the sound of the bullet and saw nothing to indicate that it was aimed at me, I dived forward and lay against the wall of the crater nearest the enemy. The hole was more than six feet deep at its center and probably twenty feet in diameter at its widest point. I turned on my back and breathed heavily.

"All those air raids before D-day may not have done much else but they gave us this," I said, referring to the shelter. Koon and Czaja grinned.

"I never heard anything in my life more beautiful than the sound of your voice," I continued to Koon. "Ever since we got here I'd been lying alone in a hole so little I could hardly move and I thought everybody had pulled out and left me."

"Why didn't you holler before? Czaja told me you were over there but I thought somebody was with you. We'd have told you to come over long ago. God, I'd have gone crazy by myself."

"I almost did," I said.

"I was alone here for a time, too, but Czaja saw me back there and came up with me. We thought until just a few minutes ago that we'd been abandoned, too."

"What's happening?"

"Nothing. Nobody can move an inch."

"We really walked into a beauty of a trap, didn't we?"

"You ain't kidding."

We were silent for a few minutes. Then Czaja said:

"You know what's the first thing I did when I got here?" I looked inquiringly. "I had to take a crap— boy, how I had to go. You know what I did?" His laugh was loud and high-pitched. "I dug me a hole right there and crapped. Boy, it was good!"

He laughed again.

"And you know what? I'm so hungry now I could eat nails. How about you two?"

Koon and I shook our heads.

Czaja shed his gear and pulled out a C ration can. He opened it and attacked the food inside with a small wooden paddle which showed from the grime of the handle that it had done much previous service as a spoon.

"Hey, don't you want some?" The thought of food made me feel slightly sick. I shook my head again. "Mighty good." He laughed. "Ah, boy, good old meat and beans. *Mighty* good." He finished, and thrust the empty can deep into the sand.

"I guess you know Laramie was hit?"

"Oh, God! No. Where?"

"In the foot. He's lucky, at that. I guess he's back on ship by now and out of all this."

"If they were ever able to get him out of here," I said.

"Oh, I guess they got him out a long time ago. He was one of the first ones to get hit when they opened up on us. They nearly got Scala, and Degliequi fixed him up, I think."

"Yeh, I saw Scala duck after they yelled for him to get down."

A machine gun burst into its rapid rattle in front of us and Czaja got to his feet and crouched, peering over the edge of the hole toward the cliff.

"Hey, Koon," he said, "I think I know where that gun is."

Koon moved over and knelt beside him.

"Where is it?"

Czaja pointed to our right front.

"Down near the bottom of the ridge. Say," he turned to Koon. "You still got those rifle grenades and the launcher?"

180

"Sure, right here in my pack."

"Why don't we let 'em have a couple?"

"You guess we can hit 'em?"

"We can give 'em something to think about."

"Well, open the pack then."

Czaja loosened the pack and Koon fitted the launcher over the muzzle of his rifle. Czaja placed a grenade on the launcher and pulled the pin. Koon thrust the butt of the rifle into the sand and alongside his right leg and held it with his right hand about the pistol grip, one finger encircling the trigger, and his left hand gripping the upper hand guard.

Czaja knelt behind Koon so that he could see along the rifle.

"Raise the muzzle a little," he said. "Now move it to the left—a little more. Okay." He tapped Koon on the shoulder and Koon squeezed the trigger. There was a dead, flat explosion and the grenade hurtled out of sight. Far ahead it exploded and we could hear the whine of the shrapnel.

"Oh, God," said Czaja, "that was way short."

"Well, let's put the next one on to about the fifth ring and raise the muzzle a little more." Koon thrust another black cartridge into the chamber of his rifle.

They slid another grenade onto the launcher and fired again.

"Hotamighty!" Czaja shouted. "That one got there, but it was a little to the left."

They fired two more grenades and the machine gun spat fitfully and then angrily in a round roll. The dirt spurted up by Koon's face and he dropped flat and slid deeper into the pit.

"Great God! We must have hit pretty close. We've got them pissed off."

"Oh, well," Czaja grinned, "that one wasn't so close to you. It's a good thing those guys can't fire a rifle."

"He wasn't too damn bad," Koon said heatedly. "He was in the four-ring, anyhow. I thought sure I was hit; some of the sand must have stung my face."

There was a sharp explosion in front of our shelter and the whine of shrapnel was blotted out by another roar, this time closer.

"Oh, Christ! We'd better get the hell out of here. They're laying the knee mortars in on us."

Czaja slid into his gear and faced toward the rear.

"I think you'd better hold it up for a few minutes," Koon said. "They'll be watching this hole now."

Czaja sank to a sitting position.

"You and your bright ideas," he said to Koon.

"*Me* and *my* bright ideas!" Koon was indignant. "You're the one who wanted to fire those grenades."

Czaja laughed boisterously.

A tremendous roar split the air behind us and we flattened ourselves on the ground until Czaja said, "That's one of our tanks," and I realized that the roar had had that double sound of the discharge and the explosion which I had noticed before. The roar came again and it was ear-splitting in its magnitude. It sounded as if the tank were firing directly over our shelter. We sat up and jammed our forefingers into our ears.

"Hell! What's he shooting at?" Czaja demanded.

As we watched the cliff the tank's gun roared again and dirt and stone spewed from the edge of the hillock (later named Turkey Knob) at the top of the ridge.

"That's not where the machine gun is," he continued. (Although it was not the location of the gun he

182

had seen, Turkey Knob later proved to be one of the strong points in the enemy defense of the ridge.)

The tank continued to fire and we watched the debris fly along the top of the high ground. And then we realized that the tank furnished us the protection that we needed to rejoin the main body of our troops. Led by Czaja we dashed out of the hole one by one and ran to the rear. We dropped into another crater and sat for a moment and Czaja ran out again. It was the last time I saw him.

To the right flank we could hear shouting and dimly we could hear the order:

"Right flank, start moving up; left flank, stand fast."

Koon and I looked at each other. He said:

"You wait here. I'm going to find what the scoop is."

He rushed out of the shelter and disappeared behind a rise in the ground.

When he failed to reappear within a few minutes I followed him but I could not see him and I found myself on exposed ground and I saw no holes which would give me protection. I turned sharply to the left and ran low until I saw a shallow, narrow trench and I dived into it. Directly in front of me lay a Marine and I could see that his right foot was torn and bloody. At the sound of my fall the man looked about and down his right side at me. It was Laramie; he had not been moved since he was shot more than eight hours earlier.

In front of him and facing in my direction was Degliequi and he nodded at me. I returned the salutation with a shake of my head and we lay for a few seconds, unspeaking, until he motioned for me to move on. I realized that I was in an exposed position in the trench.

I scrambled to my feet and started running again and this time I saw ahead of me a shell hole and I plunged into it. As I did I realized it was only a few feet from the one I had left only a short time earlier. I had run almost in a circle.

In a second crater which adjoined it lay Mikell and Meuse, members of the second squad in my platoon. With me was a man I had never seen before and I knew he must be one of the new replacements. He lay on his side in a ball-like position and he was so badly frightened that his eyes were turned back in his head and his eyeballs looked completely white.

"What's the scoop?" I shouted at Meuse.

"I don't know. They never tell us a God damn thing. All of you wait here; I'll go see what I can find out."

He disappeared toward the rear and overhead there was a burst like a clap of thunder. I looked up and saw a puff of black smoke.

"It's time fire," I told the man with me. He didn't look up. Another shell burst overhead. "I'm beginning to think those bastards want to get us." The section was getting dangerous, for time fire is shellfire with the fuse so set that it will explode in the air; it doesn't have to be a direct hit to make even the best of foxholes worthless.

A shout came from the rear. I could not understand the message but Mikell called, "We're pulling back," and to me he said, "You go ahead, Matthews; I'll come last." I picked up my rifle and sprinted for the rear.

14

They had to throw down smoke shells behind us, however, before all of us could get out and darkness had set in when we gathered at the makeshift command post on the crest of the hill near where we had started early that morning.

We were, for a short time, not an organized outfit but a frightened, milling mob. Although we did not know it at the time, our beating that day had been taken while we made our first offensive gesture against Hill 382 where some of the bloodiest fighting of the campaign took place. We already were speaking of the bottom land where we had been trapped as Death Valley and the semicircular ridge under which we had lain was the Amphitheater. The action took place slightly more than 300 yards southeast of the eastern end of the secondary runway of Motoyama airport number two and approximately 400 yards due south of Hill 382. The hill (the number designated its height in feet) was to provide us with continued bitter fighting throughout the week, but now we were concerned merely with our own plight.

Our anxiety was intensified by the fact that we did not know where our flanks were, where we were to tie in with adjoining outfits, or how our then nonexistent line would run. We knew that we should have to move quickly for now the Japs were throwing their own smoke in front of us and we were certain that a counterattack was coming.

At the same time a devastating flood of bad news about our casualties was pouring in as a backwash to our withdrawal.

"Poor J—— never knew what hit him. They blew the side of his head right off with a dum-dum. You know how a regular bullet will make a small hole when it enters and sometimes a big one when it comes out. Well, this one took the side of his head off where it hit. Blood and brains had run down all over his bazooka and we left it there but we buried the ammunition."

"C—— got it, too. He was still breathing when we evacuated him, but he didn't have a chance. Through the throat."

"And D——, I don't know where he is, but I'm sure he was dead. P——, too."

"Oh, Jesus, *he's* not dead?"

"Yeh, he died in my arms," and the speaker's eyes filled with tears, for P——, chunky and quiet and good-natured, was a great favorite in the platoon.

And the list grew larger as more units reported and the number of wounded was appalling. But the need for action finally cut short our recapitulation and a runner arrived, breathless and frightened, from the company on our right.

"Lieutenant L——," he gasped, "said to tell you C Company is dug in. . . ."

186

"This is C Company," someone said. "Do you mean B Company?"

"I guess so . . . that B Company is dug in and you can tie in your left flank . . ."

"You're over there, aren't you? You must mean our right flank."

"For God's sake, let the boy talk," Lieutenant Verica said. "You're just confusing him more."

But the boy was through talking. His face had gone completely blank and now, sitting on the ground, his head hung down on his chest and he wrung his hands nervously.

"Look," someone spoke up again, "what you mean is that B Company is dug in and we can build up with it on our right flank. Isn't that it?"

"I . . . I guess so."

And with the moon coming up high in the sky we dug in. Our squad was compressed into two foxholes. Kennedy and Deese, a replacement, and I were together and to our right was the hole containing Beeson, Koon, and Turlo. A second replacement was missing but we found him later in another platoon of our company and a third new man who had joined us only the night before was dead. Laramie had been evacuated as had Seiden, who injured his back while caring for other wounded men. Kennedy had been wounded in the arm and the injured muscle was stiff, but he refused to be evacuated.

The struggles of the day had been too much for Turlo's unhealed shoulder which now was stiff to the point of uselessness and it was evident he needed further medical attention.

The foxhole of Turlo, Beeson, and Koon actually

187

was a shelter within a shelter, for the three had dug in on the left forward rim of a large shell crater. In the center was a machine gun emplacement and on the right, another rifle position. And because of the imminence of a counterattack the word was passed that in every hole with three men, at least two should be on watch at all times and we wondered why the enemy had not hit us, for we knew that if he had struck an hour ago he would, barring a miracle, be going yet.

But now our positions were reasonably firm and overhead the artillery and mortars sizzled and this time they landed not on the other side of the deadly cliff but on this side where we knew the Japs to be; the palm thicket ahead and the denser woods on our right vibrated from the shock and danced to the ugly galloping, flaming flashes.

Although we continued to say to each other, "This is going to be a rugged night," our minds were easier, for now we were below ground and the enemy must come to us. Despite the fact that night fighting is supposed to be a Jap specialty and day fighting our *forte,* I now knew I preferred night action. The positions of the two forces were reversed. Whereas in daytime we moved against a usually invisible enemy, charged with routing him out of emplacements we seldom saw until we were fired on, now they must come to us. I had learned, too, that the enemy was not superhuman, that he possessed no special faculties for night vision, and that consequently when we were alert we almost always saw him before he saw us.

The Japanese mortars replied angrily to our barrage but they did not hit our platoon's positions and soon the counterfire died away. Off to the right in the woods rifle fire spattered fretfully and then steadily and machine guns joined in with their *nackernackernack* and then a long rattling burst and another. Somewhere along that position the slam-bang of a tank or a 75-millimeter half-track joined the fire and the tumult lasted several minutes and the flashes of mortar shells punctuated the impetuous talk of the small arms.

But in our sector we rotated the watch and in each hole one man slept and the other two fought off sleep and watched, one to the front and the other to the rear.

During my second hour of sleep, sometime during the sixth hour after we had established the watch, I was awakened by a rough blow on my leg. I did not rouse suddenly for I had fallen asleep completely exhausted and I heard dimly and from a distance Kennedy's voice:

"Wake up! There are Japs out back of us."

"There are at least four of the bastards," Deese whispered.

"Where are they?" I sat up and looked about, but could see nothing.

Kennedy pointed, but again I saw nothing.

And then in the direction of what appeared to be a pile of stones I heard a click and I saw the red-tailed arc of a Jap hand grenade in the air. Simultaneously Deese and Kennedy fired and I saw a small figure run, stumble, and collapse and from it came a wail of pain and defiance. It was in Japanese but I could tell that it was being repeated over and over again and I could make out the word "Tojo" at the end of the phrase. He had fallen behind a rise of ground which hid him from our hole but to our left and slightly to the rear another rifle slapped once, paused, slapped again. The wailing halted suddenly.

And Kennedy said rapidly and breathlessly:

"Give me a grenade. Quick. Right there."

He dropped his rifle and jerked the pin and threw hard toward the mound. The grenade roared and the fragments screamed back at us but we could not tell whether anyone had been hit. And then the air from the mound was streaked with the little red arcs so that Kennedy said afterwards it looked as if the Japs were throwing with both hands. The enemy was hidden from our position but Turlo and Beeson and Koon fired together furiously at the mound and still the grenades came over and I saw one land in the big shell hole and the cry of "Corpsman!" went up. The heavier blast of one of our grenades sounded from behind the mound and suddenly there were no more enemy grenades. An unnatural silence hung over our sector but it was broken soon down the line by the firing of other units of our company. Close to where our platoon tied in at the edge of the woods—Meuse and Mikell were dug in there—another red arc hurtled through the air, hit a tree and bounded back and exploded, and again you heard that telltale click as the Jap struck the grenade primer against his helmet and the missile threw out its spark as it went toward its target. This time a rifle barked even before the grenade exploded and the silence settled again.

Past the hole on the right I saw a figure bob up out of the ground and run stooping until it plunged into the big three-in-one shelter. It was the corpsman, who probably had been the busiest man in the platoon the past twenty-four hours. Our positions were so close together that we could hear his low-voiced instructions as he worked over the wounded. He reappeared and dodged back to his own shelter.

The attack was over, although we did not know it,

and Turlo shouted from his foxhole to tell us to maintain a watch toward the front and as the minutes grew into hours he peppered our position with rocks as a constant reminder to look to the front and not to the rear. The nervous strain added to our previous exhaustion made our fight to keep awake even more difficult than ever and we were glad when dawn came and we could move about and shout to one another.

The troops came out of their shelters slowly and cautiously in the early light and they went busily about their business of souvenir hunting. Eight newly dead Japanese lay behind our platoon sector and six wore sabers which found their way to new owners. Now the voices were free and loud.

"I hear they're going to pull us back to the rest area."

"By God, they ought to. Yesterday and last night made D-day look like a picnic."

"You know," this from a replacement, "I used to think I wasn't scared of any man or any *thing*. But I must be yellow. I was so scared yesterday I nearly shit."

"That ain't being yellow. If there's any man here who wants to say he wasn't scared I'd like to call him a liar."

"Did you see that little bastard steal my carbine last night? . . . yeh, my carbine. He sneaked up behind me and took it right out of the hole. But I got it back. I still don't know why he didn't shoot me with it when he had it . . . That's the one, right out there."

The word came to move out.

"Where're we going?"

"Back over the ridge some place."

"To the rest area?"

"Hell, *I* don't know."

The troops began moving out and litter bearers came up to the hole next to ours and removed a wounded man. Our squad stood up to get in the column of files and I saw that Koon's face and the collar and right shoulder of his dungaree jacket were caked with dried blood.

"What happened to you?"

"That Jap grenade. It landed just a few feet in front of me. I was lucky. The piece that hit me went under the rim of the helmet and got me right over the eye, but it didn't break the bone, just cut me. I bled pretty bad for a while. But God, my head hurts!"

"Who else was hit?"

"Just that one other man. I don't know who he was. He's a replacement."

"Was he hit badly?"

"I didn't have time to pay attention, but I don't think so. He was pretty bloody. But they couldn't evacuate him until this morning and he had to lie there."

We ran across the clearing until we reached the ridge. Behind it, we slowed our pace and then wound down the wire-covered path along the face of the cliff. Our company was halted at the bottom of the rise, and we took refuge in shell holes and a series of narrow communications trenches which the Japs had abandoned on D-day. We lay in the deep sand and the sun came up bright and hot and warmed us and we relaxed and talked of the night's action. Someone said:

"That was a busy night. Where'd all those Japs come from?"

"They were fewer than I expected," I said; "I was looking for a counterattack any minute."

192

"What do you mean—you expected a counterattack? What do you think all that firing was on the right? That *was* a counterattack. That's where those Japs came from. They broke through the lines for a short time and then cut over behind us. It's a lucky thing for us they didn't know where our lines were. They expected us to be along the edge of the woods but we built up right across the open. That's the reason they came trotting across that space the way they did."

"It's a lucky thing some of us weren't hurt badly, the way they were throwing those grenades around."

"That replacement in the hole with Koon was hurt badly."

"I heard that his wound wasn't so bad, that he was just pretty bloody—that's all."

"Wasn't hurt so badly, hell! The grenade landed right under him and blew one of his nuts off. Isn't that bad enough for you?"

I couldn't imagine anything much worse. I, and the others near me, fell silent. In a few minutes we saw Koon and Turlo plod toward the beach. They had been sent to the aid station on the water's edge, and this was the ninth day and three members of the original squad were left.

I had fallen asleep but I woke with the perspiration running across my face, tickling the skin as would a small insect and there was sweat running from my armpits down my sides. I removed my gear, except for the ubiquitous helmet, my combat and dungaree jackets coming off too, and I rolled up the sleeves of my flannel shirt.

I wanted to talk now, but the others about me were

asleep, and being more comfortable, I lay on my side and dozed again.

I was awakened by a terrifying thumping hiss and I flattened myself on the ground until the noise slackened and I realized that it was our rocket launcher pouring dozens of missiles over the ridge at the Japanese lines. The noise stopped but only for a few moments and then it was renewed. I jumped again although this time I knew the source of the noise. Once more it halted, then started up again. When the sibilant rush ended this time, three trucks drove away. Each bore a huge launcher on the rear and all of them were empty. They drove at a fast pace in the direction of the beach.

The Japanese, stung by the fury of the attack, lost no time in replying and now we ducked in earnest, for huge mortar shells dropped all about us and along the road down which the trucks had driven and we clung to the earth within our shelters and watched the black sand spew up and we listened to the gurgling and the whine of the shrapnel.

"This is going to be hot around here," the lieutenant said. "We'd better spread out down the hill a little way."

We waited for a break in the shelling and we moved a hundred yards away into another system of trenches.

"Why in hell don't we get out of here and on into the rest area if we're going there?"

"Because we aren't going there."

"Where are we going, then?"

"Back up on the line, but don't ask me when or where."

And so we sat and waited and we relaxed most of the time except once when a near miss from a Jap heavy mortar scattered the sand near us and the violence of the explosion rocked the earth—or so we thought until a few seconds had elapsed and the ground continued to tremble. The tremor lasted a minute or perhaps two and we looked at each other in astonishment and then uneasily.

"What in hell's that?"

"Damned if I don't think we're having an earthquake."

"Whatever it is, I wish it'd knock that crap off. I don't like it."

Neither did any of the rest of us and we wondered if we were fated to fight not only the Japs but nature as well.

It wasn't the last time we wondered that.

15

We lunged and staggered up the precarious path over the cliff again but when we were on the top we went straight to the front rather than to the right and we thought, this is better; we're going to flank the Amphitheater instead of hitting it frontally again.

We did neither. We were pulled up short and ordered to start digging. Tonight, we were told, we are going to be in reserve and we thought, this is better still. The information made us feel so much better that the inevitable scuttlebutt flowed: we're going back to rest tomorrow.

Kennedy and I were together again, this time in an old Jap emplacement of some sort. It still had three walls revetted with lava rock but the fourth, at the foot, had been bashed in by shellfire. We scooped up the loose sand with our entrenching tools and refitted the rocks into place as best we could and in a short time the shelter was ready for occupancy.

It was located between two thickets of stunted palms. To our left front was the barren terrain opening toward the front lines and we overlooked, from the right rear, another flat, barren field. Our position was to the left rear of the line from which we had jumped off only yesterday in our abortive attack against the Amphitheater. Both Kennedy and I were worried by the palm trees about us, however, and we organized an informal two-man patrol and inched through the trees until we were satisfied that at least no Japs were there before we began our watch.

But the night for the most part was quiet. Once Japs got into the lines of another outfit to our right and also in reserve and we heard the ping-whine of the bursting grenades and the shouts:

"Shoot the son of a bitch. There he goes!"

"Get him! Get him!"

And the troops left their foxholes and ran after the Japs when they fled across the field at our right rear and caught them. But after the fight was over the voice of one of the leaders—it sounded much like our own gunnery sergeant—was more terrible than the sound of the grenades.

"All right, which of you bastards was asleep and let him through?

"God damn it, don't lie to me, you son of a bitch. If you hadn't been asleep he never would have gotten to our lines. You can see a hundred yards in every direction from here. . . .

"All right—all right. But I still say you were asleep. And listen, the next time I find you asleep so help me God I'm going to blow your brains out with my own grenade!"

And once later on, when Kennedy was on guard, he saw something behind the thicket to our rear and he pointed it out to Boudrie in the adjoining hole and Boudrie flung two grenades in that direction but he wasn't sure he had hit anything.

The next morning we still clung to the forlorn hope that we should return to the rest area but deep within us we knew it to be a baseless rumor. This was the second day after the drive had started toward the 0–2 line, the day that they had said we should secure the island if the drive were successful. We knew that we were far from securing it; victory seemed almost as distant as it had the day we landed.

We were told to put on our gear and be prepared to move out in half an hour. I turned to a nearby sergeant.

"What's on for today?"

"I hate to think about it."

"You mean we're going onto the line again?"

"The word hasn't been passed definitely, but it looks that way."

It was that way. We left our shelters and went across the open field toward a ridge, and off to the right we could see the Amphitheater under which we had been trapped. We halted and separated behind two hillocks which lay below the ridge on which had been built the enemy radar station, now a mass of twisted wreckage. Across the edge of Hill 382 or Radar Hill, as it had become known to the troops, Marines already were dodging, working their way forward. Their morning's work had begun; ours, which was to be on their flank, was just beginning.

The mortar barrage which preceded our attack already had died away and the enemy had begun to answer it. Their shells fell close about us so that we curled up below the two knolls, which lay like stepping stones to Radar Hill, to await the orders to move forward.

But the order did not come. The enemy barrage increased in intensity so that the ground rocked and the air roared and the dirt flew up continuously in ugly patterns like geysers except that they spread out too wide at the base. We pressed close to the ground and scooped out tiny holes body-deep in the sides of the hillocks and lay in them that way. And the tanks came up and they, like the troops, did not venture out into the flat open field but stayed behind the hillocks with us and the mortar barrage increased in intensity and we pressed closer into the ground and cursed the big vehicles.

But we, as well as the tanks, may have been at fault, for our positions were too crowded. A well-aimed shell would have taken a fat prize, yet there was nowhere we could go for safety except back down off the ridge and we had no idea of doing that. Three of our tanks soon gathered in the midst of our troops and we were glad to go forward, for the tanks would dash to the edge of the opening, fire their double-sounding blasts in the direction of the enemy lines, and then beetle back behind the protection of the little hills and the Jap counterfire would blaze.

Precarious protection the knolls were, however, for the Japs were not using artillery against us this morning, but mortar fire. Artillery fire would have hurt us very little in our present position, for the comparatively flat trajectory would have thrown the shells either into the opposite sides of the hillocks or far over them. But the mortar fire fell almost straight down and only substantial overhead cover (we had none) would have protected us.

To the right of Radar Hill was a third knoll which would give us protection from small arms fire from the front. It would have to be the first stop on our dash to the flank. The platoon leader, the platoon sergeant, and the platoon guide set out for it on the run and our squad followed, one by one. And because we were uncertain as to the direction of the next move we began to crowd this forward shelter and we waved violently at the troops behind us to hold back and keep down. In the new position we could hear the quick rattle of the Japanese machine guns and the sharp clear crack of enemy rifles. The guide said to me:

"Run back and tell D—— to get in touch with the machine gun platoon and tell it to maintain contact with his squad and follow him closely whenever he moves out."

I bent low and ran to where D—— and his squad lay against the second ridge and I repeated the message.

"Hell, I haven't seen the machine gunners in a long time. I don't have contact with them."

I did not know whether to wait or return to the platoon leaders but I decided to sprint to the base of the first knoll which was within hailing distance of D——. There I lay in a hole which once had been an enemy shelter of some sort, probably a reinforced cave. It had been bashed in by our shellfire and our bombs. A few steel rails still protruded overhead from the side of the knoll but the roof was gone and the thick clay and stones from the hillock lay in the bottom.

Already in the ruined shelter were two Marines, one of whom had uncovered a batch of Japanese letters and a note book whose pages looked as if the former owner had been a correspondence student in geometry. The Marine stuffed the letters into his pocket for delivery to his platoon leader.

The others dashed across the open space and crawled into the hole but with five men it was crowded and they edged out with the statement that they were going behind the ridge and wanted to be called if the others moved out. And the mortar fire increased and fingered out toward our shelters and we lay close to the wall, hoping none of the shells would make a direct hit or land against the face of the knoll.

I heard my name called and looked out of the shelter. D—— beckoned to me and I ran to his position.

"Tell Summers," he said, "that I've contacted the machine gunners and that they are moving up. I've told them to keep in touch with my squad when we move out."

I repeated the message to him to make certain I had it correctly and raced around the edge of the hillock and toward the one behind which the platoon leaders lay. They nodded when I delivered the message and Boudrie said:

"We'd better start moving up now," and he motioned to the man at his side to lead the way. The man crouched at the edge of the knoll for several seconds.

"You'd better get a move on. We've got to shove along."

The man looked over his shoulder and grinned nervously.

"Don't rush me."

He peered cautiously into the open, rose from his knees and broke into a sprint, running with his knees well up, like a trained athlete. He raced in the direction of the northern rim of the Amphitheater, which lay about a hundred yards away.

"Oh, for God's sake," Boudrie moaned, "he's going in the wrong direction."

He walked to the place from which the other man had started his run.

"I tried to tell him that our lines would be in that direction." He pointed at an angle of about 30 degrees to the left and turned to our squad. "Do you see that tank?" We nodded. "There's a hole directly behind it. Run until you get there, then cut to the left. Hold it up along there until I get the rest of the platoon moving and I'll come up and give you the scoop from there on. Now take off."

One after the other we began running, bent low and weaving. Somewhere to the right a machine gun stuttered at us and we raced into the first hole we came to. We were breathing hard and we lay on our sides against the front edge of the hole and waited for the firing to stop. We scrambled over the edge and ran again until we heard other small arms fire and in this way by short fast sprints we arrived behind the tank. We lay there longer, for the sand of the open field was almost as deep as that of the beach and the effort of pulling our feet loose from the suction was sapping not only our strength but our nervous energy.

Again we moved, now to the left, going by ones and twos, and this time other men from another outfit were there in the hole to which we had been told to go and when we rushed in they scowled.

"Oh, God, here they come! Now we'll get this place nice and full and they'll rain mortars all over us. Why in the hell don't you guys hold it up?"

We stood at the edge of the hole and when we saw someone start up from the shelter we had just left we waved violently and shouted for him to go back. It was a useless effort for on no occasion did one of the runners see us until he had advanced to such a place where turning back would have been more dangerous than advancing. The men were being ordered to go forward and it is doubtful that they would have held up in their old positions even if they had seen us earlier.

Boudrie slid into the shelter to direct our next moves but before we could go forward the familiar rumble told us that a tank was coming near. It stopped close by and it attracted the usual reception. Enemy small arms fire died away magically but the mortars redoubled their efforts until the tank backed up and disappeared.

The understanding, or even the knowledge, of tactics still was beyond our simple province but we knew two things: we were moving around the right side of Hill 382 and, from the left, by-passing the Amphitheater—no more frontal attacks there, thank God! If it could be cut off from the remainder of the Japanese forces it could be cleaned up with comparative simplicity. We did not realize yet the bitterness of the resistance on the hill itself; we were still obsessed with the thought that the semicircular ridge on our right constituted the main resistance on this front.

Boudrie told members of the first squad to follow him and he edged over the forward rim of the shell hole and ran toward the line of trees in the distance. He took cover after traveling about fifteen yards and told us to wait. He disappeared toward the front and a short time later we heard his shout. We moved along the path he had taken; it was not difficult to follow for we could see the heads of Marines forming a haphazard line in the craters before us.

We were, Boudrie told us when we arrived, slightly out of position.

"Do you see that first tree out there?" He indicated a point about fifty yards away to the right. We did. "We've got to pass the word back for the rest of the fellers to head in that direction. They needn't come up this way; they can go straight out from where they are."

We darted across the open space and the small arms fire which had been vigorous though sporadic since the tank left now blazed into violent action. We holed up near the first tree and shortly afterward the first of the men from the rear began to arrive. Back in the direction from which they were coming we could hear the dread call for the corpsman. . . . Someone had been hit.

And as the men from the rear began to arrive we pushed forward, slowly and in small dashes, for the fire was too heavy to allow sprints of any distance. And again we began to collide with rear units of other outfits, and they, like the first, cursed at our coming for they were piled against their forward elements with nowhere to go.

Boudrie, with Drinnon the runner close behind him, scouted out to the left front and he returned with the news that all outfits in front of us had been pinned down by a machine gun to the left and that no line had been formed with groups which were supposed to come behind the Amphitheater from the right. We would have to sit tight. And although he did not mean this literally, tight was how we sat—tight against the ground.

The small arms fire continued viciously and it was joined again by the burst of mortar shells which probed about dangerously among our shelters and we could do nothing but lie there and take it. But the problem of halting the flow of men toward the front again was pressing and we shouted and waved for those behind us to hold up. It did no good. Members of the second and third squads came up and then other platoons began to overrun us and the heavily loaded men of the machine gun platoon staggered into the hole and cursed at the crowded condition and sought other shelter nearby. Strays from other companies and even from another regiment found our crater and we felt that it must somehow be magnetized to draw so many men.

It was a deep hole, and wide, but we knew it was far too crowded for our safety and we shouted ahead to find out if there was room there for us. Usually there was not but occasionally the word came back that there was "a little" and by ones and twos we would trickle forward and soon those holes would be overcrowded. And we knew that as long as the units in front of us were pinned down we were pinned down, too. But soon it became even more elemental than that, for the snipers and the machine guns began to concentrate on our own sector and we ceased to think in any terms except of the here and now.

It seemed as though the enemy were laying down a sort of zone fire to prevent our moving, for, even when we were well protected in our craters, the bullets would bite across the rims, spurting the dirt into the air. But the Japs weren't just zone firers. Contrary to everything I had heard about them from veterans of other campaigns rifle-proud veterans who scoffed at their ability to shoot—these were accurate marksmen, deadly accurate. And the ugly word of casualties flowed among us again and the feeling of impending disaster was heavy in our minds.

The hole in which I took shelter was in reality three craters which flowed together almost in a straight line. At the forward end the crater was almost deep enough to allow a man to stand in its center without being seen and the pit at the rear was approximately four feet deep. The two were connected by a shallow hole which was about six feet long but hardly two feet deep. Kennedy and I lay in this corridor side by side and face down, our cheeks pressing into the sand. When we smoked, as we seldom did, we scooped the sand away from our bodies so that we could reach into our jackets rather than lift our bodies off the ground.

It was during a lull in the firing that Corporal G—— of the first platoon came to the shelter. We waved him in from where he sat on the edge above the corridor and he crossed it and went into the deepest crater and took a seat along its side. His head barely protruded above the rim but someone said:

"You'd better get down, G——; they've been . . ."

There was that three-dimensional sing-crack-bop of the Japanese rifle and G——'s head fell heavily to one side, jerked once, and fell again. Blood spurted from his nose and his mouth.

The men near him sat motionless for a moment. It was obvious that G—— had died instantly. His body retained its sitting position and only his heavy hanging head suggested the grotesqueness of death.

"For God's sake, somebody cover up his head."

A man near him opened his poncho and threw it over the dead man's head so that his shoulders and body remained exposed. We continued to cling to the ground and to hope that the jam ahead would clear up so that we could move forward. It is easier to attack than to withdraw.

But when the word finally came, the news was that A Company, into which we were to tie, had lost heavily under machine gun and mortar fire and had been unable to make contact at its right. Without a solid line in back of the Amphitheater it would be impossible for us to stay there and a withdrawal had been ordered.

Our company was to hold its position, we were told, until A Company removed its wounded and then withdrew the survivors. After that a progressive withdrawal would be effected with those units nearest the front moving out first. The laying down of a smoke screen in front of us would be the signal for the movement to begin.

Information seeping back down the line said that A Company's heaviest casualties had been caused by a valiant but vain frontal charge against a blockhouse. We understood later how that could be, for on subsequent days, direct fire from the 75-millimeter cannon of a tank failed to dislodge the enemy from his position and the blockhouse finally was destroyed only by a vicious dive-bombing attack.

And while we lay there the sizzling of shells over our heads began, followed by the flat thuds of their striking. The smoke had started. But a high wind was blowing and by the time the smoke had gotten to us it was no longer a screen but merely a discoloration of the air. Nevertheless the evacuation of the wounded began and stretcher bearers streamed into and out of our position and I marveled that so few of them were struck, for it was impossible for them to run with their heavy burdens in the deep sand.

The remainder of A Company moved through toward the rear and we followed them, returning over the same route by which we had come. When we stopped at the large hole which had been so overcrowded it was almost empty. Three wounded men lay in the bottom of the crater and a single corpsman

208

worked over them. He said two of the casualties would be able to walk to the aid station with assistance but that the other would need a litter.

The smoke died away and on its heels came the increasing spatter of the enemy small arms fire and we cursed the gunners back of us although we knew the failure of the screen was not their fault. Because of the wind the shells, to be effective, would have to be put in one particular sector and Martel was sent ahead to the command post to ask for stretchers and "more smoke, more smoke, more smoke around our positions."

And suddenly in intervals between bursts of fire we heard a wailing shout to our left and in the direction of the Amphitheater and all talking stopped as we listened. We could not understand the words and the voice had an eerie, ascending note.

A Marine stood up.

"Get down!" someone shouted at him. "That doesn't sound like a Marine. It may be a Jap trick."

"Shut up and let's listen."

The voice died momentarily and then shouted again, stronger.

"Help!" it shouted and then it called a name.

"By God, that *is* a Marine. We've got to go out and get him."

"Hey, come back here. S—— went out that way to get somebody just a few minutes ago and he had just stuck his head out of the hole when he got one straight through the forehead."

"God damn it, we can't just let them stay out there for the Japs to get."

"But we've got more casualties than we can handle right now. We can't afford to have any more running out in that direction and getting shot up."

"Yeh. For God's sake, use your head. It's better to lose one man than a dozen trying to get out there. Let's play the percentages."

" 'Play the percentages,' hell! Suppose you were lying out there; you wouldn't give a damn about percentages then. F—— you and your percentages!"

"But I tell you we can't take care of any . . ."

"Oh, for Christ's sake, shut up."

Corporal Foster, a replacement, stood up.

"I'm going out there. Who'll come with me?"

"I will," said Degliequi.

Foster left his Browning automatic rifle with the man at his side, crouched below the lip of the crater for a few seconds and then sprinted into the open. He ran toward a hole which we had left only a short time before and then cut sharply in the direction from which the voice had come. Degliequi ran directly toward the left.

In a few minutes he reappeared.

"It was a Marine, all right. There were three of them. They're all lying out there in a shallow ditch and they can't walk. They've got to be carried. Foster's waiting with them."

Foster's voice floated back now:

"Send somebody out to help me carry one of these men."

"Hold it a minute," Boudrie shouted. To us he said: "There's no use in trying to get them out by hand. We've got to have stretcher bearers. There aren't enough of us to get them all out and we can't be running back and forth unless we get more smoke. . . .

"Come on in," he shouted at Foster.

"I need help," the voice came back.

"Tell those men we've got to get more help. We're

not going to leave them out there. Come on in now. We've got to get going.''

The smoke shells were falling with a new intensity when Foster reappeared. Stretcher bearers with one litter had arrived in the meantime and they started back with the wounded man in our hole, and members of our platoon, including Meuse and Mikell, lifted the other two casualties to a half-walking, half-dragging position and staggered into the open.

We waited until the casualties had a chance to reach shelter and Boudrie said:

"All right, let's go."

This time we did not wait to go out by ones or twos but we clambered out of the hole and sprinted across the open together, scattering as we ran, and the rifles and machine guns spoke behind our backs and spurred us on.

We made our way down the face of the ridge, slumped over and silent. The wounded men had been evacuated and a check had showed our own casualties had been comparatively light and our feeling of expected disaster had slipped from us. But now we were gripped by exhaustion, a terrible exhaustion which turned our muscles to jelly and buckled our knees. And because the fatigue was nervous as well as physical, we were seized also by an apathy which obliterated everything but the harrowing necessity of picking our feet up and putting them forward.

Lieutenant Verica, his left sleeve slit to permit the dressing of an arm wound received during the afternoon, led the way and he stopped by the company dump where men shouldered a box of C rations and a can of water.

From the foot of the ridge we headed across the open field toward the positions we had held last night. That, at least, was one thing: we'd be the reserve line for tonight so we should be able to get some sleep. The very act of walking was torture and midway across the field my head swam and the ground whirled and I stopped short and leaned on my rifle for a moment until I could see clearly.

The foxhole I had been in last night looked wonderful. I propped my rifle in a corner, stepped into it, and allowed my knees to buckle. I fell on my face and then turned on my back, content in the soft sand.

Kennedy, who had brought the C ration box, dropped it at the foot of the hole and sat beside it. I wasn't interested; I was beyond the state where food could help me. Someone put the can of water at the edge of Boudrie's hole near ours and most of the platoon gathered to refill their canteens but again I could make no move. It would be there when I wanted it.

Off in the distance, seemingly in another world, we could hear the *whee-ee-eet—whee-ee-eet* of the Japanese rocket bomb which we sneeringly called the buzz bomb and the moaning Minnie. And none of us cared, for we heard it every day about this time and it was almost laughable the way they would toss a shell over near the airport, then the next might hit the beach and the next fly completely over Suribachi and land in the ocean. It seemed to be as purposeful as lightning and we feared it no more than we should have feared a thunderstorm. And again we heard the *whee-ee-eet—whee-ee-eet* on the ascending scale and those at the water can and the ration box continued to resupply themselves.

And the earth threw me into the air and my vision

grew black and something fell across me and it was a man and somewhere in the void someone screamed. Then there was absolute quiet.

There were no more screams, but the silence was broken by that more terrible sound, the moaning of the frightened, the wounded, and the dying, and the moaning was at first soft and then rose wordlessly to a crescendo. The man lying on top of me rolled to one side and rose to a half-sitting position. It was the lieutenant. He gasped and then said:

"Can you reach my first aid pouch?"

He looked at his hand the fingers of which were torn jaggedly.

I opened the carrier and the container within it and I stood up.

"Who's up there?"

I looked and told him.

"You'd better look after him. Just open the sulfanilamide for me."

I got out of the hole. The man was lying just outside and his feet were dangling over the rim. He moaned horribly and he clutched at the ground with his fingers and rubbed his face back and forth across the sand. A great hole almost the size of a man's head opened below his belt and above his hip and I noticed that his canteen was gone from one of his carriers but the cup was still there and because his cartridge belt had been blown below his hip the cup was half filled with blood.

I tore open his first aid pouch and I realized suddenly that I was acting stupidly. It was useless to put sulfanilamide on a wound of that size for the immediate danger facing this man was not infection. I opened the battle dressing to place it over the wound in an effort to stop the flow of blood and I realized that

that, too, was stupid for the dressing was only a small fraction of the size of the wound. It would merely have dropped uselessly inside.

Drinnon ran over by me and I told him who the man was and he said, "We've got to get him out of here right now."

Each of us seized him by an arm and the wounded man moaned horribly so that we put him down, and we knew we must have hurt him terribly, but it was the only way we knew to get him to medical attention for we had no stretchers.

In the distance I saw the battalion command post and I told Drinnon I would get help. I ran across the field and it seemed to have grown to an endless width and I ran until I tripped and fell and without rising I shouted and waved my arms.

"Corpsman! Corpsman!"

"Do you need a corpsman over there?"

"All you've got, and stretchers and ambulances."

They wasted no time racing across the field and they had caught up with me before I got back to our area.

Someone said:

"You'd better put out that fire; it'll just draw more shelling."

I noticed for the first time that where the rocket had struck just outside the scrub palm thicket at the rear of my hole a spreading circle of flames licked over the dry grass and bushes of the area. We went back and stamped the fire until our feet were hot within our shoes and the fire was out, and then we returned to the area where the wounded men were lying.

For the first time I saw Kennedy again. He was standing watching a corpsman apply dressings to a man, both of whose arms were hanging by threads of skin. Close by another man stood and his right arm was dangling so that I knew he would lose it but he seemed uninterested in it. He was twisting his left hand in front of his eyes curiously and I saw that one finger had been torn as cleanly from the hand as if it had been cut off by shears.

"Are you hit?" I asked Kennedy.

"I'm not sure, but I think I must be. My shoulder feels funny."

He turned his back and I saw a hole in his jacket and I helped him take off his gear but he would not put it down; he insisted on retaining his cartridge belt and his gas mask and he clutched them to him with his right hand.

He slipped out of his jacket and I saw that he had a T-shaped wound in his shoulder.

"You'd better get it fixed up. I think they're bringing an ambulance up here."

Without a word he turned and walked to the rear.

But the ambulances did not come and the men called for them in piercing, loud voices until Lieutenant Davis, First Battalion adjutant who had come with the corpsmen, said sharply:

"All right, now. Let's knock off that screaming. You're not doing any good; you're just working everybody up. They'll bring the ambulances as soon as they can."

An ambulance came and stretcher bearers moved toward it with the man with the wound in his hip. He had been stripped of all his gear and, now composed but pale and unspeaking, he clutched tightly to him the Jap saber which he had captured two days before.

And Drinnon said to me after he had gone:

"Both he and — were begging us to shoot them."

The survivors stood about looking stunned except for two or three who wept and shook convulsively.

The wounded and the dead had been removed and the missing men searched for briefly and we gathered our gear and headed back across the field but this time to the right.

Our plans had been changed.

We went back into the line and dug in across the right flank of the third platoon and during the night three more from our platoon cracked up and were taken, shaking and sobbing, to the rear.

16

That was the night we dug into the hot ground and again we wondered if we were going to have to fight nature as well as the enemy.

The gray sand on the top of the earth was so hard that we had to turn it with picks before we could spade it out but six inches below the surface it was heavy and coarse and a crumbling black. As we knelt within it our knees grew warm and then uncomfortably hot. I thought at first we might have dug in on a freshly spent piece of shrapnel and I put my hand down and burrowed into the earth but as soon as I touched it I knew the sand itself was hot.

And then I noticed that as we dug, the freshly turned earth steamed and I looked along our line and discovered all of the holes looked like simmering kettles in the moonlight.

I remembered that Iwo was one of the Volcano Islands and I knew now that the group was not misnamed. I should not have been surprised at any moment to see lava begin to flow.

It was not lava, however, but subterranean sulphur

springs and nothing happened except that when we lay down in our foxholes to sleep we sweated profusely but when we arose to take over the watch the chill wind whipped about the upper portions of our bodies; our rumps and legs sweltered while our heads and shoulders were chilled.

Only that happened . . . that and the fact that the Japanese mortars including their heavy, which was three times larger than our biggest, laid down their fiercest night barrage of the operation, so far as our company was concerned.

We were delayed in pulling out in the morning for we had to reorganize. The second platoon ceased to be a platoon; it became merely one squad in the third platoon. It was not a full squad at that for it had only two groups instead of three. The reorganization brought home to us more than anything else the cumulative effect of what we had undergone. Not until now had we realized the number who had been killed or wounded or were missing or had broken under the strain. They had gone at first a few at a time and then last night the horror and terror of the catastrophe had dulled for us its full implications. There was no walking about in the open, no shouting this morning. We sat in our foxholes knowing nothing and expecting everything and nothing.

We began to move toward the ridge again after the sun was well up in the sky and the Jap snipers were not content to wait for us on top of the rise today. One of them was firing steadily at us when we peered out of our foxholes. We left our shelters as we had moved out of the craters on the ridge yesterday morning: by ones and twos and on the dead run.

The two replacements in the hole with me started off

first and I followed them. My pack, my rifle, my head, my arms, all seemed to hang on me with great weight and the night's rest had not dissipated my exhaustion at all. Indeed, the inaction had seemed to have an adverse effect, for my feet, which had been treated when we were in rest area, were stiff and sore, and the right one felt as if it were split across the ball. Even so early in the morning I was compelled to duck into a shell crater about twenty-five yards away and rest. A——, who had come into the squad last Sunday, knelt there ahead of me, his face buried in his shaking hands. He was weeping.

"Are you hit?" I asked.

And then I noticed that the top of his helmet was ripped away along a line about three inches long and pieces of the inner liner protruded above the steel.

He shook his head and said nothing. There was nothing I could do for him so I merely said, "Take it easy."

But he rose suddenly to his feet, turned to his left, and plunged out into the open. The last I saw of him, he was running in the direction of the aid station.

It was mid-morning before we were atop the ridge today and we moved with a caution which was quite unlike even yesterday's slow beginning. At that time it had been a slowness born of uncertainty of terrain and direction. But today we knew the terrain as we knew the touch of our helmets on our heads and we knew where we wanted to put our line. We were slow now through caution.

We sandwiched the replacements in between the old men—that is, the men who had come through the first ten days of the operation—and we cautioned each other constantly to maintain contact from front to rear and to avoid overcrowding of shelters.

We were tense from our experiences of the last three days and a replacement and I lay in a shallow hole against the second hillock and were silent as we awaited the word to go forward. Once again I heard that short, sharp sibilant and I pressed myself close to the ground and waited for the shell to explode but it did not. I realized that the hiss came from the replacement who had sighed and blown his breath into the sand by my ear.

Waiting was the hardest of all.

About five yards away lay Mikell and Drinnon and I kept my eye on them for it was from them that we should get the signal to go forward. They, in turn, watched to their front, but no signal came back.

The acting company commander passed by and he said to us:

"You people all right?"

"Yes, sir."

"Then why aren't you moving up? Where's the rest of your outfit?"

We pointed to Drinnon and Mikell.

"The rest of the outfit has moved," he said. "I think you've been left behind."

He walked over and talked with Drinnon for a few minutes. Drinnon, who until today had been a runner, had been transferred to the platoon because his experience in three previous operations was needed badly on the line. As calm as if he were walking in his own yard, he rose and strolled into the open field and to the next shell hole, a huge Japanese saber dangling from his back.

In a moment he had returned. It was true; we had been left. Contact had been broken almost as soon as the precautions were issued. One after the other we moved forward.

Locating our squad was easy. We merely ran from shell hole to shell hole in the direction of the disabled tank, and in the movement we found release from the strain which had afflicted us as we waited. But it was not movement alone. The strain had stayed with us yesterday afternoon. It was the movement in addition to the mental exhilaration of going forward and we lacked the depression which was caused by the withdrawal.

We found the squad in the large crater near the disabled tank. Although it had not progressed half the distance gone yesterday it already had overrun elements which should have been in front of us. Someone was pinned down ahead; therefore we were pinned down here.

The crater was large and our squad was small and we were not too crowded but in spite of this the enemy snipers and machine gunners already had sighted in on our position and the bullets whistled and cracked overhead and I could tell that the sniper fire came from the right side. It sounded as if one of the machine guns fired from the same direction—probably within the Amphitheater—but the other apparently was located to the left in Hill 382 behind the collapsed radar equipment.

Wherever they were located, they were effective in keeping us down and once more the feeling of desolation which had come over us in the triple crater yesterday settled on us.

Again, too, we heard the rumble which could only mean that a tank was coming from behind the knolls to our rear. It moved in our direction and stopped only a few yards from our hole. One of the men in the squad looked up and said:

"Oh, Jesus, here we go again. This is going to be just a carbon copy of yesterday."

But this time it was different. The tank sat there a few minutes, then it moved out into the open field to the left and where it had been another came and this one continued to the right and a third pulled out into the open.

The mighty wham-bang of the tank guns roared out on two sides of the hole and the enemy's small arms fire decreased and then died away. The third tank was within view of our hole and its turret swung around like a mighty head looking for something it could devour. The roar of the tank guns continued but now it came from different sectors of the field and you could tell the vehicles were firing as they moved, making themselves more difficult targets for the enemy mortars.

But the mortar fire began to drop. Today, however, the Japs had three dangerous adversaries rather than one and they made no hits and the shells fell at a distance from our shelter.

Drinnon watched the tank nearest us for a few minutes and then he rose to his feet.

"You know that machine gun over there that had us pinned down yesterday?" he asked the sergeant who was acting platoon leader of the third platoon. "I believe I know where it is. How about this?"

He talked to the sergeant for a few seconds in a low voice and then he ran into the field and behind the tank. He opened the telephone box, pulled the instrument out and crouched under the vehicle talking.

In a few seconds he was back in the shell hole and he

222

put his rifle aside and removed all of his battle gear except his helmet. The motor of the tank roared and the vehicle backed along the sand in the direction of the hillock and Drinnon raced after it. Under the protection of the knoll he clambered onto the tank's top and lowered himself through the turret. The motors roared again and the tank moved out into the open and its guns joined in the attack against the enemy.

And as we watched rear elements began to crowd in on us and we shouted and gesticulated to those back of us to hold up their advance but they continued to come, not in a mass, but singly or in small groups which were, nonetheless, as irresistible as a tidal wave.

When our tank returned to the shadow of the knoll and Drinnon left it and returned, the crater was crowded almost to its edges and the sun already had begun to descend in the west. Again the only choice was to move forward and many members of the platoon to which I now belonged were sent to the next crater, approximately twenty-five yards away and past the disabled tank, with instructions to stand by there until we received further orders.

The active tanks continued to fire for a short time and only occasionally did a daring enemy machine gunner rattle off a burst in our direction but the mortars continued to play over the field about the tanks and the shrapnel whined over our heads.

My friend from boot camp, Ray Marine, was in the hole and with him was his tentmate, Hartman, and we chatted and tried to joke.

"Something's wrong here."

"What's that?"

"I mean something must be mixed up. This is the

day we ought to be off the island. Remember? Five days to secure it and five days to mop up.''

''Yeh, and not more than two days on the line.''

''Maybe somebody forgot to tell the Japs about it.''

''I think I'll go check in now and tell 'em the ten days are over and I'm going in.''

It wasn't very funny, but it was the best we could do and for the most part we lay on the sand with our eyes closed and some of the men dozed and one, in the bottom of the crater, even snored gently. And Marine and I shared our cigarettes because both of us had few and neither of us knew when he would be able to get more.

We went through the formality of offering each other smokes but neither of us would accept from the other and it always ended up with the one who lighted it taking two or three puffs and passing it to the other and it would go back and forth between us in this fashion until it had reached finger-scorching proportions.

But soon everybody had dropped the pretense of trying to be funny and a boy near me said, almost as if to himself:

''Do you ever think you won't come out of this alive?''

''I've thought that every day this week,'' another answered, ''ever since we started banging up against this ridge.''

''You know, I can't quite figure out how we still *are* alive.''

''Yeh, it ain't much fun to start out in the morning telling yourself, 'Well, this is it; this is the day I get it. I can't miss today.' I think it every morning while we're waiting to push out. There's just one good thing. . . . As soon as we get started, I'm all right. It's just the looking forward to it that gets you. As long as you're going, it's okay. By God, it's just when you get into a place like this that you start thinking again."

We fell silent again but now were utilized only sparingly the cigarettes and the water and the conversation.

In the distance the roar of the tanks' guns grew more sporadic and the sound of their motors indicated they were pulling back in our direction. One of them passed by our hole and continued toward the knoll, but the other moved to a short distance away and stopped.

There was almost no fire for a few minutes but the ground suddenly rocked and a geyser of black sand spewed up a short distance to our right. Everyone in the hole was awake immediately. The shell had hit so close there was almost no sound of the flying splinters.

"That son of a bitch!" someone shouted. "I guess he's going to sit there until he gets us all blown to hell."

"Oh, Christ, this place is going to get too hot again. Let's get out of here."

Our hole trembled again and to our left this time we saw debris flung into the air in the direction of the disabled tank. One to the right, one to the left . . . where would the next one be?

"Let's get out of here," said Hartman. He and the remainder of his squad disappeared in the direction of the first knoll.

We sat huddled in the bottom of the crater a moment.

"What do you think? I know we were told to stay here until we were ordered out, but I don't think they meant under conditions like this."

"I don't either. I think we ought to get the hell out."

One at a time we headed toward the hole from which we had come. Those who had preceded me were in plain view past that crater when I came across the top of our shelter and out into the open. I ran fast and low, swerving as I went, and again I had the feeling that enemy snipers behind me were waiting for just this opportunity.

I dashed into the big hole but none of the platoon was there. No one was there except six dead Marines, and I realized that the second blast must have been a direct hit in the crater. I paused a few seconds to catch my breath and plunged on.

The platoon was behind the second hillock when I arrived there and they were working on the wounded. Our squad was decreased again. Drinnon, whose fine work in the tank had ended such a short time ago, was unscratched but as badly hurt by concussion as he would have been by the shrapnel. He sat wearily against the side of the knoll, completely unaware of what was happening about him.

And on his helmet lay a large clot of another man's brain.

Before we dug in that night we heard again the shrill ascending *whee-ee-eet—whee-ee-eet* and we scrambled almost madly to nearby shell holes and dived in and piled one on top of the other, but the rocket did not strike in our area.

Later the word was passed by telephone that we should go onto the ridge again in the morning and somewhere along the line a man sobbed when he received the order.

We quit our foxholes before dawn and we were ordered to move up by infiltration: that is, individually and rapidly and unobtrusively. It was the way we always had moved atop the ridge but it was the first time that it had been thought necessary for us to infiltrate to get to the crest.

The day had broken when we reached the last of the knolls which stood as protection between us and the open field across which we should have to run and one by one we ran, dashing across the ruts which the tanks had torn in the deep sand and toward the shell holes and the disabled tank. And even as I crossed the ruts a bullet tore into the ground before my feet and I slid into a crater nearby and crouched for a few seconds.

I resumed my run toward the hole behind the tank but the mere coming up the ridge this morning had exhausted me and my run, as on the first day, had slowed almost to a walk by the time I arrived.

Most of the squad already were there and the others came shortly after I sat down on the slope of the crater above the bodies of five of the six dead Marines. Our attitude toward the bodies was almost perfunctory; we were neither particularly curious nor did we disregard them in the way we might have earlier, in an effort to avoid the ugly situation. For these were not men we knew; they were the result of man's ferocity and we were used to ferocity now.

"We will," the acting platoon leader said, "begin building up our line here. This hole will be the anchor of our outfit. You two," he pointed to Deese, the replacement, and me, "will stay here. You will stay here until we give you the word to move up, and you will make contact with Able Company moving up from the rear. The rest of the outfit will be in the next few holes

227

ahead and we'll give you the word when we start moving."

Again using tactics of infiltration, the remainder of the platoon darted into the open, taking the now familiar route which we had crossed and recrossed previously in the week. And the intermittent sniper fire was padded out with the rattle of the machine guns, and mortar shells again began to fall in our area.

Deese and I looked at each other.

"How long do you think we'll be here?"

"There's no telling. At least until A Company makes contact with us, I suppose."

"I don't like that damned mortar fire—not after what it did to this big hole yesterday."

"I don't either. I'd feel a lot better if we were dug in."

"Hell, let's dig."

We took turnabout with the one entrenching tool we possessed, although Deese did the major part of the work for now another trouble plagued me. The thumb which had been slightly red a few days before now ached so viciously that I could hardly grip anything with the whole hand. Under the filth, which undoubtedly had aggravated the condition, the skin was tight and hard and gray with an infection which had spread from the tip of the thumb to a point near the second knuckle.

However, we managed to dig a foxhole near the rim of the crater and, if the legs of one of us were crossed over those of the other, we both could squeeze into it. It was almost no protection but we felt more secure in the face of the intensifying mortar fire.

We were hungry, but there was no food and we were also starved for the taste of cigarettes but almost all of these were gone and we smoked sparingly as the minutes built into hours.

In the din of the firing we could hear no calls from the men ahead of us and when the time came for the platoon to move, Mikell had to leave his shell hole and race back across the open to notify us and the three of us dashed forward together, forgetting the infiltration tactics. Awaiting us was Meuse, Mikell's close friend and tentmate, his clear cut features drawn and inconceivably filthy, and I suspect we all looked that way to each other. It was Meuse whose flat New England voice had lashed the men into forming stretcher parties to remove the wounded men from below the knoll where they had been taken after the shell hole had been struck yesterday afternoon.

Our advance again was delayed for a short time and we had just begun to move when two men, obviously replacements, dodged across the edge of the hole. One of them cried sharply and fell, pressing his hand to his hip but his companion, who stuttered badly—I don't know whether it was from fright or naturally—looked at him and hoisted him to his feet.

"It's aw-ll right," he said. "Y-you're just ni-ni . . . nicked in the b-butt."

We turned to the left and dashed toward the tree line along the edge of the ridge, the ridge that overlooked the valley where we had been trapped on Monday; we began again to collide with troops established in the craters along the route. They were members of Able Company which was supposed to have made contact with us earlier, but they had missed us by going in front of the disabled tank rather than behind it as we had done.

They cursed us as we slid into the craters with them

and they warned against overcrowding and we moved on for we had no intention of staying. We were supposed to be ahead of them. We moved up past our farthest point of previous advance and cut sharply to the right and entered the woods in the rear of the Amphitheater.

We took refuge in what probably had been a well-defended Japanese emplacement, the walls of which were revetted with the thick lava stones. The platoon command post was there and the acting platoon leader spoke over the portable radio.

"We're in position in the woods. Baker Company is on our right and it's trying to make contact with —— Company," which was from another regiment, "on its right. When it does we'll have a line all the way across the ridge and then I think we'll be able to start advancing. . . . Out and over."

The air sighed and we doubled up and pressed close against the sides of the emplacement but the sigh continued and we relaxed and looked about. The battered branches of the trees waved in a gentle wind.

We moved out again, this time in pairs and with me was Sergeant Summers, always as calm as if this were just another maneuver. We bent low now as we ran, for the warning had come back that snipers lay ahead. We saw none and we resignedly expected to see none for, except at night, few of us had glimpsed a Japanese since we had come onto the ridge the first part of the week. This realization was not a thought then; we were too seriously engaged in a desperate race. But the word, race, is not to be confused with speed. Although I *was* in a race, and with what I considered potential disaster, my mind was again heavy with the realization that I was losing. My muscles refused to function properly after the first few steps and I was occupied with the grim business of trying to coax co-operation from my legs. I lost, and my run turned to a hectic, straining trot and just when I knew I should fall from my own efforts, I slowed to a walk, feeling angrily ridiculous in my ineptness. Summers already had reached the next cover but he refused to take advantage and turned, instead, with his head well above ground, to watch my progress anxiously. The location of the position was accented by the sergeant's presence and I fixed my attention on it greedily and forced my will to lift my feet, for even the tiny undulations of the almost level ground now were making me stumble.

I arrived at the edge of the crater and moved over it and my mind heard again the things my concentration had stifled—the slap of a machine gun and the angry detonations of mortar shells.

Our shelter now was in a hole which evidently had housed an enemy mortar crew. Empty shell cases, bearing Japanese characters, had been piled to one side but the stack had collapsed and the containers lay about the bottom of the pit so that we had to restack them before we could sit down in the hole with our heads below the rim. I leaned back, exhausted. Summers watched me steadily for a few seconds, offered me a cigarette, then deliberately turned his attention to his rifle.

A corporal from the third platoon, followed by my friend Ray Marine, dropped into the hole and spoke to Summers:

"Mikell just hurt his leg. Fell and twisted it pretty bad and passed out. I told him to go back to the aid station. That all right with you?"

"Sure. I'm glad you did it."

231

Now only Summers, Meuse, and I were left of the original platoon which had hit the beach on D-day.

Marine, his usually husky frame almost cadaverous from fatigue and hunger, shoved a shell case away and sat beside me. The movement of the box released a strong stench of human excrement and we arose, examined the ground under us and sat again, cursing the filth of the enemy. Marine and I shared the cigarette, for he also had no others. I loosened my cartridge belt and settled back, and then I noticed that he wore no belt. Instead, he carried his canteens in the pockets of his dungaree jacket and his ammunition was borne in two bandoliers which crossed his chest. He explained that he had taken off his heavy gear and left it at the command post the day before, in order to join a stretcher party removing wounded. When he returned to the c.p., his gear was gone, and this was all he could find. We lapsed into silence.

Sergeant Kinnally, the acting platoon leader, appeared.

"Baker Company has made contact with —— Company. We've got a line across the ridge. I've told the Beaver"—the front-line nickname of the acting company commander, Captain Helton—"and he says we're going to get an artillery and rocket barrage and attack that ridge over there at 1315. We haven't got much time so stand by to get going."

He moved back to the temporary command post.

"So we've finally put a line across this damn place!" exclaimed a third platoon member.

"It looks like it," Summers replied.

"By God, that's something. We've been trying it for five days and finally we've succeeded."

"Now we'll really start fighting. They say they

captured two Jap prisoners who told them that ridge is the main line of the Jap defenses. When we get there they'll throw everything they've got at us until they wipe us out or we wipe them out."

That, too, was a fable, for the enemy played it smart and did not throw away his troops in the old violent counterattacks. But we didn't have a chance to find it out then for Kinnally was back.

"Baker Company just passed the word that it doesn't have contact with —— Company anymore. The bastards have pulled back . . . Christ, don't ask me why; I don't know. All I know is that Baker Company says they've gone."

The sizzling of our artillery shells overhead already had begun and now came the dreadful thumping hiss of the rockets and we watched them arch far overhead.

"It's time for the advance to begin. We've got to tell the Beaver about this business. We can't go forward without a line."

The feeling of frustration closed on us until it was almost physical. I again unbuckled my belt, which I had fastened when we were preparing to move forward and I leaned back and to one side, so that I rested on my elbow. The movement seemed to have sapped the last ounce of my strength.

Summers watched me again for a few seconds. Then he said:

"Report back to the c.p., the battalion c.p.—do you think you can find it?—and tell them I sent you back to rest for a day or two. Find Gunny Lewis and maybe he can get you something to do, but get a good sleep. We're going to have to do a lot of running around up here, so you'd better go now."

I arose, adjusted my gear and picked up my rifle. We

said "take it easy" to each other and I climbed out of the shelter and headed toward the rear and the route going back looked longer than it had coming up. I proceeded in cautious, short dashes to the nearest craters and the farther I traveled the more pronounced became the old familiar sense of despondency at withdrawing. My exhaustion pulled at my legs again and when I slowed down to a walk my knees buckled. When I reached the shell hole near the ruined tank I felt the other familiar sensation: *this is what the snipers have been waiting for; you're in the center of their sights.*

I scrambled out of the crater and ran across the last long stretch of open terrain and my run turned to a shuffling walk and I crossed the ruts which the tanks had worn in coming from behind the razorbacked hillock and I tried to lift my feet but they were heavy, too heavy, and I tripped and fell. I crawled behind the knoll to safety.

The men sitting there were mute and uncomprehending when I asked, "Where is the First Battalion c.p.?"

I turned to the jeep driver, working to unload mortar ammunition from his trailer.

"Do *you* know where the First Battalion c.p. is?"

"You bet. Hell, I'm going by it in just a few minutes; just hop in the seat there and I'll be ready to go in a few minutes."

I couldn't hop. I crawled into the seat and braced my aching right foot against the fender.